The life of a
SCILLY
SERGEANT

Sergeant Colin Taylor has been the longest serving police officer on the remote and tranquil Isles of Scilly for several generations. Over the years his regular blogging about the unique policing exploits there was enjoyed by millions worldwide. He has now returned to the relative simplicity of policing on the mainland UK. This is how he survived.

T0158608

The life of a
SCILLY SERGEANT

COLIN TAYLOR

arrow books

7 9 10 8

Arrow Books
20 Vauxhall Bridge Road
London SW1V 2SA

Arrow Books is part of the Penguin Random House group of companies
whose addresses can be found at global.penguinrandomhouse.com.

First published in Great Britain in 2016 by Century

Published by Arrow Books 2017

www.penguin.co.uk

A CIP catalogue record for this book is available from the British Library.

ISBN 9781784755157

Typeset in 11.02/15.00 pt Electra LH by Jouve (UK), Milton Keynes
Printed and bound in Great Britain by Clays Ltd, Elcograf S.p.A

Penguin Random House is committed to a sustainable
future for our business, our readers and our planet. This book is
made from Forest Stewardship Council® certified paper.

For my dad
Michael Charles Taylor 1939–2014

CONTENTS

DEAR READER

Congratulations on picking up a copy of my book. In just a short while you will be reading about what it has been like for me as a police officer on the Isles of Scilly.

I can say with some level of certainty that I am the longest-serving police officer on Scilly in peacetime, having been posted here for seven years in total. This is an easy claim to make, however, as Scilly also happens to have been at war longer than any other place on earth – other than the Netherlands, with which she was at loggerheads for some 335 years, the longest conflict in world history. It kicked off when, in 1651, Admiral Maarten Harpertszoon, of the Dutch Navy, got uptight and testy over some boating issue while he was visiting Scilly. I suspect he was denied local rates on a return ferry crossing to St Agnes from St Mary's for an evening meal at the Turks Head, or something similar. This war, like most disturbances I have dealt with here, was a benign affair. Not a drop of blood was spilt nor a single shot fired, but the Admiral died years later without either side having backed down on whatever had upset them in the first place. It wasn't until 1986 that local councillor Roy Duncan stepped in as the man of the peace and suggested everyone calm down and let bygones be bygones. A truce was declared, with a deputation from the Netherlands visiting Scilly to shake hands. The Dutch have slept soundly in their beds ever since. There are, however, now no local rates on the inter-island ferry crossings. Thanks for nothing, Maarten.

The point of this observation is to highlight, in context, how easy it can be to upset people, especially in a small community like the one I patrol, and how that upset can have lasting consequences. Some also consider it important to recognise and respect that places have their own culture and customs. I consider myself in that number. I am conscious, too, that I am a serving police officer. Not many coppers with a desire to continue their careers write books about their beats. I have no axe to grind and only fond memories of my time here. I would also like to be able to come back on holiday in due course without having to sport a false beard and dark glasses or waving a white flag and peace treaty.

With this in mind, and to spare blushes, I have taken steps to change or omit some of the names, places and details, in the hope of protecting the identities of certain individuals – which is a difficult task in such a small place, I can tell you.

In 1829 Sir Robert Peel, who established the British police as we know it today, set out his nine Peelian Principles of Policing (yes, they are for real), the seventh of which I am particularly mindful of in the context of this book. It is as follows:

Police, at all times, should maintain a relationship with the public that gives reality to the historic tradition that the police are the public and the public are the police; the police being only members of the public who are paid to give full-time attention to duties which are incumbent on every citizen in the interests of community welfare and existence.

So anyone could have written this book, basically, but as I wear a silly hat and epaulettes, and for many years have managed the Isles of Scilly Police Facebook page, I got there first.

In being part of that 'police are the public and the public are the police' thing, I have adopted some local terms in a subconscious effort to blend in and avoid faux pas; you will find many of these terms sprinkled throughout this book. The definitions of some of them are a bit of a movable feast. As such, a certain mystique is preserved about the place, which can never be categorically exported to the mainland. There I go – I have already started to talk in local-speak, introducing the term 'mainland' like a throwaway comment. I'll therefore start with that:

GLOSSARY OF SCILLY TERMS

MAINLAND

The mainland is everywhere in the United Kingdom that is not Scilly. Scilly has never, to my knowledge, been connected to the mainland by any form of land bridge, and indeed even the glaciers of the Ice Age came to a halt just before reaching the island shores, leaving the archipelago basking in a tropical maritime temperate zone ever since.

The islands have always been islands. This is why there are no large land mammals here like deer, foxes and badgers. We do enjoy the chilled-out sunbathing Atlantic grey seals that haul their blubbery frames out of the water to catch the rays on some of the rocks around the coast. The most famous of these is Stinkweed, a large, distinctively spotted bull who is so unfazed by life that many snorkellers have risked hypothermia just to bob about at the Eastern Isles next to him. He and his lardy harem, though, cannot really be called land mammals. Hedgehogs were only introduced in the 1980s, smuggled in a suitcase or similar and released by someone playing God. They bred like they were on a cheap sun-and-sex holiday in the Mediterranean before, in a cute Beatrix Potter way, they set to chomping their way through the native flora and fauna.

As a group of islands, Scilly is separated from the rest of the United Kingdom by a stretch of very chilly Atlantic. Only one person has ever been reckless enough to swim the twenty-eight miles between Land's End and St Mary's. Everyone else flies or sails. It would be nice to be able to confine 'mainland' to a simple geographical term, but it is more loaded than that. The noun 'mainland' can also be used as an adjective and is slightly derogatory. It confers a singular lack of competence to whatever is under discussion. 'I am going to the mainland' means what it appears to mean. 'It's a mainland law' casts a dark storm-cloud over that piece of legislation, with a mountain to climb for whoever has the task of enforcing it.

ISLES OF SCILLY, SCILLY, SCILLY ISLES, SCILLIES

This is where the uninitiated could really trip up. It's possibly where the Dutch Admiral went wrong in the first place, is my guess. If you want to blend in like a native, refer to the archipelago as the Isles of Scilly. It is generally recognised that this can be a bit of a mouthful time and time again in normal discourse, so it is acceptable to refer to the islands as just plain Scilly. No sniggering. It may be pronounced the same as 'silly', with a silent 'c', but giggle at your own peril. Nor is it Sicily, which has considerably more takeaway pizza outlets, Mafia and donkeys. Some people who do not have the travel knowledge to make the distinction between Scilly and the football off the boot of Italy are gushing in their praise for our grasp of the English language, believing that we must all be native Italian speakers. These people invariably work at call desks for car insurance companies and fail, also, to comprehend that complimentary home-start plus roadside recovery and a courtesy car is not a big selling point for their product on islands with a maximum of eight miles of metalled roads and only golf buggies to hire.

Referring to this place as the 'Scilly Isles' is considered poor form and draws a sharp intake of breath. Worse still is to call the islands the 'Scillies'. You might as well start a war. Get this right from the offset and you have a chance of blending in and going unnoticed.

OFF-ISLANDS

This refers to the inhabited islands of St Agnes, Bryher, Tresco and St Martin's. St Mary's, the largest of the five inhabited islands, is referred to as the Main Island. The off-islands are a further step back in time from even St Mary's, which itself, in my view, seems to enjoy a feel of the mid-1960s. The off-islands are very different from one another in appearance and character, and visitors seem to decide upon their favourite in an even spread, according to variables like abundance of beaches, rugged-ness, sophistication, isolation, exposure and history. I have no favourite. I have often thought about this, and each time I 'go off-island' (away from St Mary's to one of the off-islands) I find that my destination becomes my favourite for the day. I do have a favoured pub, but that will remain a secret.

SCILLONIAN, ISLANDER, OFF-ISLANDER, RESIDENT

Dare I say it, but the definition of Yorkshireman sets the standard as the simple way to define a person's heritage. If you are born in what they term 'God's country', you are a Yorkshireman/woman. If you choose to leave, you remain a Yorkshireman/woman. Very simple to apply and under-stand. It is not so simple here. Scilly is where God comes on holiday to get away from it all.

If a person lives on Scilly, they are a resident. On this basis alone they are not considered Scillonian. If a person is born and lives on Scilly, they are an islander. On this basis alone they are not a Scillonian. If the place they live is on one of the off-islands, they are an off-islander. They are still not a Scillonian.

If they were born on Scilly, as were their parents, and all of them have lived there, they are still not a Scillonian.

The perceived wisdom is that a person's grandmother has to have been born on Scilly for that person to claim some level of credibility when calling themselves Scillonian. I am sure that in another generation a person will have to hail island ancestry back to great-grandmother, and so in this respect new-family-name Scillonians are always a vanishing prospect.

Early on in my time here I once asked a self-declared dyed-in-the-wool Scillonian what defines him. He looked at me and said, 'It can all be summed up in one simple joke. How many Scillonians does it take to change a light bulb? Change?' From that I took a fairly stubborn independence to be a strong defining feature.

One thing is for certain: Scilly is not Cornish. I'm very fond of Cornwall and all that – lovely pasties and clotted cream – but Scilly is not Cornish. Scilly has its own flag: it's orange and blue with a white cross and stars. There is no discernible accent on Scilly. A bit of a Cornish twang for some perhaps.

Most residents of Scilly are blow-ins and castaways from the mainland who pitch up, find and fill a niche and make a living. Many wear several hats to make ends meet.

Fisherman/builder, farmer/shopkeeper, boatman/painter: the mix is extensive.

I am at best a resident. Like all the police here, we blow in for a brief few years and then get shipped back out to the mainland to let someone else apply their own take on law enforcement.

VISITOR

A visitor is one who comes, experiences, goes and hopefully comes again. Visitors build up a wealth of knowledge about the islands over the years, which often surpasses that of those who live here. They are like stalagmites: grounded from the roots of their first trip, familiar and slow-growing. Their knowledge is one of facts, figures, history and local personalities. They have their favourite haunts and habits. They develop a preference and enthusiasm for certain boatmen to transport them between the islands, for example. They frequently have a favourite island or restaurant. 'Visitor' is an affectionate term for people who are the lifeblood of the islands. Without visitors, Scilly would be a very different beast, for 83 per cent of the islands' income is derived from the visitor trade. Quite simply, without visitors the islands would be made up of distant frost-free flower farms, with a few crabbers and lobster potters. The whole year is geared towards the receipt of visitors. The year is less about the changes in temperature than it is about the ebb and flow of visitors. On patrol, I meet hundreds of them.

TOURIST

This term is rarely used by anyone on Scilly outside tourist marketing agencies. A 'tourist' conjures up an image of a camera-clad individual with a bucket-list of venues to attend and entrance fees to pay. While Scilly is stunningly photogenic, it is without doubt lacking National Trust properties, cathedrals and theme parks. The bucket-list of a satisfied visitor pretty much consists of ticking off the five inhabited islands, and seal- or puffin-watching trips. Tourists are busy people, maximising their brief stay in a place. The experiences and offerings on these islands do not lend themselves well to a holiday frenzy. The slower way is de rigueur. Learning to walk again, and re-training the eyes for long vision, results in a successful trip. Fast and furious tourists are prone to be disappointed.

THEFT AND BORROWING

The Theft Act 1968 is very clear about this distinction. If you dishonestly take something that belongs to someone else and you do not intend to give it back, that is theft. Borrowing is what you do when you ask a neighbour to lend you their lawnmower, for example. Where this all goes awry, however, is in applying it on the streets here on Scilly. Taking someone else's bike from where it is leaning against a wall in town, and pedalling it up Church Street after closing time, for instance, is theft. Realising I am in hot pursuit in full uniform, then pulling to a stop halfway up the street to let me catch up and very compassionately asking 'Are you all right, Colin?' as I am bent double, gasping for breath, wheezing like a sixty-a-day smoker and looking like I need a defibrillator, lessens this to taking without consent. Most of the islands' other inhabitants call it borrowing, but the expectation will be that I will still chase the borrowers.

Walk out of the Bishop and Wolf pub, half-cut, on stellar course to effect the perfect crime of hot-footing it with the 50-pound cast-iron admiralty anchor directly in front of the islands' police sergeant, and it is debatable whether you had any intent other than to slip a disc or sprain a muscle. There is no speedy getaway with an object the very purpose of which is to root something to the spot. Indeed the best option when you spot the looming form of the officer on duty is to simply turn full circle and lug the item back into the pub, apologise to the landlady and go home quietly. Which is what happened. I considered this to be less an act of villainy and more a reckless excuse for a day off work to see a chiropractor. There were some who viewed this as a stocks-and-rotten-fruit matter, but as long as I have equal numbers of people at any one time complaining I am too lenient or too harsh, I figure I have pitched it just about right.

There you have it: your basic starter kit for survival on Scilly. The rest you can pick up along the way. I think this is sufficient training for me to be comfortable taking you on patrol with me around my beat.

WELCOME TO SCILLY

Rounding the corner to the slipway outside the Mermaid Inn, I saw a circle of twenty or so people standing in the almost pitch-dark. The only light came from the wind-blown swinging pub sign, fixed high on the wall above them. They were facing inwards, excitedly observing an event in their centre. It reminded me of a gathering outside the gates at the end of school. All that was missing was the chant of 'Fight, Fight, Fight!' It was evident they were marshalling, as best they could, a disorder that was brewing in their midst and were stalling for time until the cavalry arrived. The heads turned towards me as I ran into view. I was evidently that cavalry – an army of one. Whoever amongst the group had made the call could be forgiven for not being impressed with the show of strength from the constabulary. This matter was mine to sort out, and mine alone.

Who should I deal with first?

The actions of the surrounding crowd of pub customers answered my question, the instant I arrived. They burst apart, like a speeded-up time-lapse film of a lotus unfurling.

There in the centre was the business end of this hellish flower: a five-foot six-inch, late-forties brick outhouse, a labourer known to his mates on-site as 'Sweetcorn'. The previously hemmed-in, drunk-and-disorderly builder was funnelled by the crowd on a trajectory towards me. It felt like pass-the-parcel, in a game where nobody wanted to unwrap the next layer because everybody knew there was a crap present inside. Sweetcorn pointed at me and spoke in his best Bob Hoskins, East London accent.

'You had better get out of here, or I'll put you on your arse.'

A greeting no doubt calculated to shatter any illusions I might have had that the man with the incongruous nickname was interested in forging an enduring friendship. To be honest, adding another person to my Christmas-card list was not a priority at that precise moment in time. Staying alive seemed a more pressing concern, judging by the look of aggression on Sweetcorn's face. The instant I arrived, I was the focus of his attention.

It does not take too much skill to draw such attention. The uniform does the trick, all too often. The uniform has a gravity that encourages inebriates either to become aggressive or to start up uninspiring and poorly timed conversations about a long-held dream to embark on the same career path.

'I always wanted to be a police osiffer. What do I have to do, to join?'

'Sober up is a good start.'

On this occasion, the human being squaring up to me was clearly not asking for a job interview. As he was currently only twelve feet away, my training told me that I had about one or two seconds before Sweetcorn could close the gap and reach me from a standing start. This large, angry man already had momentum, however, and the laws of physics were not going to hinder him in his mission to close the gap even sooner. It was quickly apparent to me that rapid tactical communications, in the form of a little fancy footwork, were going to have to play a significant part in ensuring that we both made it to the next day unharmed – a day of sobriety, when Sweetcorn could perhaps regroup and focus on developing a mutually agreeable relationship with me.

I backed off, to give myself some time, and to give him a visual clue that I posed no threat. I told Sweetcorn to calm down, but he kept coming. He was now six feet away. I was convinced he was going to assault me, and I was unconvinced that I could fight him off by hand, and felt I would have to resort to something from my range of personal protective equipment attached to my jacket. The top-of-the-scale options were my baton or pepper (Captor) spray. I am trained in both. Every year, in every police officer's career, we are given refresher sessions in the use of our equipment and the safe handling of the person we have used it against. The idea is always to use the least-harmful method to bring the drama to a safe resolution for everyone. The least-harmful method is often simply officer presence. That alone calms many situations.

It clearly wasn't working in this instance. Nor was the next option: talking. And I was going to lose in an all-out fist-fight or wrestle, so I was going to have to take things to the next level – the Captor spray. (As an aside, I have never had to resort to use of my baton in twenty-one years.

Well, that is a lie actually. I did use the heavy butt-end of it once, to break a window when someone asked me to, as they had locked themselves out of their car. But I have never swung it at a person.) Captor is more commonly known as 'pepper spray', as it contains the active ingredient from capsicum chillies. That's the bit that incapacitates. It wears off in a short while, but for the first few minutes it stings like buggery, completely distracting the attacker and allowing time for them to be handcuffed and calmed. Sometimes that is all an enraged person needs – a break in their hysterics, so that they can snap out of their moment of red mist.

I reached for my pepper spray to the right-hand side of my jacket. My hand closed around it and, as I drew out the can, my thumb popped the flip-top lid, exposing the red deploy button. Raising the aerosol to point it directly at Sweetcorn's face, which was looming large on my horizon, I took a step back and, as I pressed the button, stumbled over one of the wretchedly quaint heritage cobbles that made up this part of the road. A stream of capsicum shot out into the void, mostly missing its intended target. In trying to regain my balance, I lost my grip on the can and it fell to my side on its elasticated bungee rope and danced around my ankles like a failed yo-yo. Sweetcorn kept coming, and I swear he licked what little pepper spray had reached his lips and widened his eyes with an expression that conveyed: 'Well, what you gonna try next, Sweet Cheeks?'

I kept backing off. With a level of futility, I did the only thing I felt able to do in the circumstances and called for help on my radio.

'Charlie Whiskey one-two-four.'

'Go ahead, one-two-four.'

'I need urgent assistance.'

'Where are you, one-two-four?'

'Scilly.'

Silence.

On the mainland an emergency call like this would prompt other police officers from an impressive circumference to pipe up on their radios with confirmation that they were racing to help. Not so, on Scilly. I have made this shout twice in seven years out here, and both times I got the distinct impression I was being listened to with impotent but curious concern. 'How's he going to get out of this, I wonder?'

Think of the pregnant pause that Houston gave, on hearing *Apollo 13* transmit that it had 'a problem' in 1970. There were striking similarities with the brief radio silence I experienced.

The islands here are, at their closest, twenty-eight miles off the tip of Land's End. England is closer to France at Dover than Scilly is to Cornwall. There is an open expanse of Atlantic Ocean that is uncrossable in a meaningful timeframe at night, unless you have a military helicopter at your disposal. I knew nobody with that capability would be listening in, but felt the need to remind my colleagues monitoring the radio waves that my enviable posting to paradise came with the caveat of isolation. Comms broke the silence after what seemed an age, but was in reality only a second two.

'One-two-four, what do you suggest?'

'Call Mat at home. Wake him up. Tell him I'm gonna

try and bring in a prisoner. I'm about to get into a fight. Gotta go.'

I felt in those few seconds that I had been ignoring Sweetcorn for too long, and I didn't want to upset him further. Abandoning the respectful silence on my radio, and still backing away from the angry man, I grappled for the springy elastic cord that my pepper spray was dangling from and retrieved it, like I was pulling up a wriggling mackerel. All the time being subjected to a tirade of threats from the man looming large over me, which I resolved to survive, and refresh Sweetcorn's memory with, once he was nursing his hangover.

This time the aerosol worked. A short half-second burst sent a jet of stinging pepper spray into his face. It stopped him in his tracks, which is what it was designed to do. Imagine scratching the tear-duct of your eye after chopping up those tiny Scotch-bonnet chilli peppers. The realisation of your mistake comes on quickly. You can't open your eyes, and for no explicable reason your tongue comes out, as you try to blink away the pain. Now magnify that tenfold and you come somewhere close to understanding the discomfort Sweetcorn was in. The spray would wear off with no lasting effects, but for the fifteen minutes of his disablement, it put me in a position to take hold of him and tell him he was being arrested for disorder.

Sweetcorn struggled a bit and, to my relief, several of the crowd that had been standing around pitched in and helped me handcuff his hands behind his back, before an enthusiastic posse of them accompanied me and Sweetcorn on the short walk back to the police station. To Sweetcorn's credit, he did calm down very swiftly. The moment had passed and he was into what I would term his 'moment of clarity'. Comms had evidently raised Mat and he was unlocking the police station, rubbing his eyes to wake himself, having been roused from a deep sleep minutes earlier.

Four minutes before meeting Sweetcorn for the first time, I too had been fast asleep. Safe in my own bed, warm under the duvet, lying next to my wife, happy and snug in the land of Nod. Probably dreaming; certainly not anticipating meeting a construction worker before dawn. In those intervening four minutes I had to wake, answer the phone, take in directions, get dressed, dance the quickstep with the cat at the top of the stairs and race down the road to speed-date a man I had never previously met. It was the dig in the ribs and a grunt from my wife, the lighter sleeper to my side, that prompted me to pick up the ringing phone on my bedside table. This did not fully wake me, however. For what seemed an age, I struggled to understand the significance of speaking on the phone, in whatever cosy dream sequence REM-sleep had put me in.

It is always like that for me, when woken in this fashion. It must be very strange, and not lacking in humour, for the radio operators who have to call sleeping policemen, to hear them groggily coming out of whatever childlike or sordid dream sequence they are committed to. The echo of the large room in which the caller was speaking, and the sound of other operators talking calmly and entering details 'tappety-tap-tap' onto their computers, came slowly into focus. These clues told me that this call was unmistakably from a call centre. The professionally apologetic, but urgent, 'moving on swiftly' tone of the male voice addressing me confirmed that my caller was a radio operator at Devon and Cornwall Police, Plymouth Control Room, as opposed to a PPI call from an impersonal droid somewhere on the planet.

'Hello, Sarge. It's Comms at Plymouth. Sorry to wake you.'

'Errr? . . . No . . . that's all right. What time is it? What's up?'

'Yeh, sorry, but we are going to have to call you out. It's twenty-three minutes past midnight. There is a fight at the slipway near the Mermaid public house in Hugh Town. The caller has asked that police attend – two men are fighting. Can I book you on? Do you want to go on your shoulder number or your call sign?'

'Errr . . . What? Fight? . . . Err, I'll take my call sign. The Slip, you say?'

'Yes, Sarge. Do you know where that is?'

'Yes, of course. It's just down the road. I'll get dressed and get my kit and make my way there. Book me on as Charlie Whiskey one-two-four.'

'Yes, will do. Let us know when you get there.'

'OK.'

I hung up. Awake now, I slapped both cheeks to wake myself further and get into character. No longer horizontal in the foetal position, I was a vertical policeman again.

I dressed in a hurry in the dark. I don't switch on the light to get dressed when I am called out, as a small marriage-enhancing consideration to my still-sleeping wife. Once I was sure I had my top and trousers on the right way round, I stumbled downstairs, using up a life each for both me and the cat in the process. Recovering my balance,

I cursed, before finding and lacing up my boots. I ran down the path from my house to the police-station entrance, a forty-yard dash around the other side of the building from my front door.

I had to go to the station first to get my kit on. I needed my radio, stab-jacket, pepper spray and handcuffs. Seventeen pounds of Kevlar and fighting irons, in a black webbing waistcoat that gives the wearer the flexibility of a fully robed geisha, but with none of the beauty. I bound myself up in my ballistic straitjacket. Fleetingly I considered leaving my custodian helmet – such impractical headwear for running or fighting in – but I had a particularly shocking case of 'bed-head' and, even at moments of pressure like this, a little vanity creeps in.

It made sense to cover the distance to the disorder on foot. The police Land Rover was pointing in the wrong direction and, if there is any single fault with a Defender, it is that it has the turning circle of a supertanker. A three-point turn would take too long. I was in a hurry; it would be quicker on foot. Plus the fact that the run would wake me up and make me less fuzzy, for the task of managing a situation that could amount to somebody – me – getting hurt. I had only been awake for less than three minutes by this stage. At a jog, the scene of the disturbance was just over a minute away. No point in trying to break the 400 metres world record. Arriving bent double, wheezing and in need of a defibrillator, does not inspire confidence.

As I approached, I could hear the sound of aggressive shouting from what was clearly an excitable, alcohol-fuelled situation just out of sight. I continued round the corner onto the slipway. This was when I saw the crowd, and when they looked up to see me arriving to tackle 'Sweetcorn'. This was also when my brain chose to amuse itself with my ridiculous predicament: what on earth was I doing? Forty-six years old, on a remote island in the Atlantic, outside a pub after midnight, about to enter into a scuffle with a fifteen-stone inebriated brickie? If I died now, would the coroner report the fact that I had tartan pyjamas on under my uniform? What had become of my life? How did I get here?

HOW *DID* I GET HERE?

My journey to Scilly started with an evening of romance. Sarah and I got into a mood with each other, driving home from Exeter after fish'n'chips at Harry Ramsden's, followed by *The Full Monty* at the Odeon. I have no recollection of what the disagreement was about or who started it, but the food and the film were both good. The pitch of our angst increased throughout the drive back to our home on Dartmoor, so much so that I overshot our house and drove a couple of extra miles onto the moor, before pulling over into a lay-by. It seemed like a good idea at the time, and has since proven to be one of my best. I didn't want to take our anxiety into the house. Paper-thin party walls in our cob cottage would broadcast the trivia of our relationship to our neighbours. This had to be quashed in the car, and an unremarkable muddy gateway in the rain along a high-hedged lane in west Dartmoor was as good a place as anywhere. I needed a plan that would bring this brief moment of joint madness to a happy conclusion. I needed it rapidly, before it escalated beyond my control.

I cut the argument stone-dead with an unrehearsed but

long-overdue proposal of marriage. No bended-knee stuff. No ring in a box. No flowers. No asking the father. Just crash-bang-wallop: 'Let's do this. Marry me!' Sitting, seatbelts on, both facing ahead through a rain-splattered windscreen with the intermittent wiper action going on a dark night in November, in a muddy gateway in the middle of Dartmoor. It worked. Sarah accepted. Killed the argument stone-dead. Sweet!

In June a year later we tied the knot and resolved to honeymoon in the UK. We were not afraid to travel; both of us had been to numerous ports in far-flung places, but we settled on a set of priorities. There had to be no uncomfortable searing heat, no long-haul flight, no currency conundrums, no mosquitoes. Most of all, we insisted on the simplicity of speaking our mother tongue. It had to be exotic, though. We had both heard of the Isles of Scilly and knew they were somewhere near us in the West Country; but, given a drawing pin, I'm not sure we would have stuck it accurately on the tail-end of the UK, just off Land's End. Somewhere off Cornwall, we guessed. Most certainly a bunch of islands, but how distant we had no idea. Let's call it an archipelago. People lived there at least some of the year, we were guessing. Was there a bridge to get there by? Should we sail or fly? Could we drive when the tide was low? No idea. In 1998, before the Internet as we now know it, it was a matter of going down to the travel agent's and getting a brochure full of pictures and telephone numbers. Scilly ticked all the boxes. What with our love of the coast, seabirds, salt water, seaweed, sea fishing and boating (did I mention the sea itself?), it was a given that our once-in-a-lifetime, two-week honeymoon would be off the tip of Cornwall. Lots of telephone calls later to various guesthouses on different islands, we had our honeymoon sorted.

We opted for the boat – the *Scillonian III* – a sharp, white destroyer-shaped ferry that cut its way from Penzance thirty miles out into the Atlantic to St Mary's in two-and-a-half hours. The only ferry to Scilly, and foot-passengers only. The enhanced pitch and roll of this shallow-draughted ship ensures it has a motion that has caused some cruel folk to give her the sobriquet the *Sicklonian*. She is built that way to enable her to berth at the shallow ports of both St Mary's and Penzance. I have travelled on her many times and have never once felt the ill effects.

I'll spare the full details of the two glorious weeks we spent on Scilly. Needless to say, our three-island June stay was magic. We took in lodgings on St Mary's, St Agnes and Bryher, with day-trips to Tresco and St Martin's, assisted by a scorching summer. We did all the dreamy 'what if?' stuff that great holidays are all about. It was also a relaxation for me to be distracted from the focus of being a new in-service Neighbourhood Police Officer at Burnthouse Lane in Exeter. Two weeks off-duty in an obviously crime-free paradise by the sea – marvellous.

The very first day back at work after the honeymoon, I found myself in the parade room at Heavitree Road police station in Exeter. It was late summer 1998. As we prepared for the shift ahead my colleague, PC Rich Newton, scoffingly chucked the internal job bulletin across the room at me. 'Here, Loverboy Taylor. There's a job for you on Scilly. They want a PC out there, a.s.a.p. You could have another two years on honeymoon.'

Not everybody gets two bites at the same cherry, especially when that cherry is both of the best policing jobs in the world. The first bite was the one pitched to me by Constable Newton. I successfully landed that Police Constable post on St Mary's and held it for the full tenure of two years, from 1998 to the summer of 2000. The second bite was eleven years later when I was by then a Detective Sergeant at Exeter CID.

My day-to-day work involved managing a team of detectives. We investigated burglaries, assaults, sexual offences, drugs, robberies and almost any other matter that generally left misery, lives changed and invariably would end up in Crown Court. I had been a detective since returning from Scilly, the first time around, and had been promoted to Sergeant in 2004. In that intervening time Sarah and I had got busy and made a couple more humans that we named Lewis and Isabella.

I liked being a detective. It was a sideways move and a specialism, like being a Traffic officer, Firearms officer or a dog handler. It can be a permanent career choice for some officers. There is no hierarchy between specialists. We all have a deep, healthy respect for the job that the other person does, while at the same time gently ribbing each other for their alternative career choice. In the end the only real difference comes down to how and where we take our coffee. Detectives drink in the company of others from a favourite mug at their desk; Traffic officers drink with their crew mates from cheap paper cups at service-station car parks; and dog handlers drink alone – except for a panting canine with a one-syllable name – sipping from a steel flask in the middle of a muddy field. The combined effect of our efforts aims to hold the baddies to account, and to provide justice to those who are vulnerable. Detectives generally do not wear a uniform, just so that there is never the prospect of having to stand in that muddy field, drinking an inferior brand of instant coffee and getting dog-slobber on our trousers. The detective role is better suited to smart plain clothes, and the tastebuds to a sensitive blend of Robusta and Arabica. As I say, theoretically there is no hierarchy; it's just a matter of our outlook on life. Suited and booted sometimes makes for better managing the sensitivities of vulnerable victims and witnesses, too.

In 2011 my children were too young to have seen me in a police uniform up to that point. They knew that I was a policeman, but had no real idea of my job, outside what they would pick up from TV or books. I remember one day, just as I learnt of the advert for the Scilly post, I was dispatched from my office to a murder scene. I had to hold the fort and supervise the other officers and the scene until the senior officers arrived. We blocked off the road around the premises with police tape. The body of the victim still lay inside the house at the centre of the cordon. The suspect had been arrested and led from the house as I arrived. The local press turned up just moments after I did. The photographers immediately started snapping away, to get a clichéd picture of cordon tape and uniforms, for the morning's paper. I was the only suited police officer present inside the cordon. I saw one photographer go for his camera and point a telephoto lens at me, just as I took a call on my mobile. He must have been thinking it was a great shot of the steely-eyed detective at a murder scene, talking on his phone to Crime Scene Investigators and feeding back pertinent details of the dramatic event. If only he knew the exact nature of the call.

'Hello – this is DS Taylor.'

'Hello, Daddy.'

'Bella, I'm at work. Is it important?'

'Daddy, I helped Cathy dag sheep after school.'

'Bella, I can't really talk about this now. Can you tell Mummy that I will be late home. I'm at a job.'

'What's happened, Daddy? Is it gory?'

'Bella, I have to go now. Just tell Mummy. I'll hear all about the maggots when I get home, if you are not asleep.'

This was the exact moment the camera shutter captured the case-breaking detective in action. It made the pages of the *Exeter Express & Echo* the next morning.

I was not really looking for an escape from our village or from my job, but on seeing the advert for the post of Police Sergeant for the Isles of Scilly, I couldn't put out of my mind the urge to return – and take my family with me this time. I didn't mention it to Sarah for the first few days. I needed to be sure in myself that it was a level-headed move. However, with the deadline for applications fast approaching, I broached the subject one morning in the car on the weekend shopping trip to the supermarket. To say that Sarah was as enthusiastic as I was would be an understatement.

'The job of Sergeant on Scilly is up for grabs. Shall we?'

'Yep.'

Not a second's hesitation from her. I think she even bought packing tape, in readiness, on that trip to Sainsbury's.

Generally an advert for a police job on Scilly is not well subscribed. It is no surprise to me that so few people actually apply for a posting out here, when the posts come up. On first appearances, either of the policing roles on Scilly – be it Constable or Sergeant – sounds like just about the best posting anywhere in the world. The successful applicant gets accommodation, no commuting and enviable levels of autonomy, within the confines of the law and police procedure. All in beautiful surroundings in a low-crime area. What's not to like? Closer inspection, however, reveals that it means being away from family and friends, sometimes stranded there, depending on the weather. If the partner of the officer has a job, he or she may have to give that up. There are no prospects of promotion while in post, and the isolation is not for everyone. There is no large shopping arcade, cinema or ten-pin bowling on Scilly. Correction: the New Inn, Old Town Inn and Seven Stones Inn do screen films from time to time, but I fear it will be a wait before we see our first red-carpet event on the isles. You make your own entertainment.

There does appear to be quite a culture of drinking out here, though. There are five pubs on St Mary's, and one on each of the other islands. During the spring and summer they do good trade and in the winter, when the visitors have gone, it tails off. The main supplier of food, the Co-op, has a very busy alcohol section in its floor space. In rough seas, when the supply ship cannot make the crossing, the shelves run bare of meat, bread, veg, fruit and milk; but pop in for chocolate or a bottle of wine, and there will be ample supplies. The Canadian Ambassador to the UK visited Scilly once and, on leaving, quipped that he found it to be 'two thousand alcoholics clinging to a rock in the Atlantic'. He was wrong and exaggerated for effect, but it would be inaccurate to maintain that alcohol does not feature as a strong theme in this community. Some people may observe that it is pretty rich for an ambassador to be so critical of alcohol consumption, when diplomats are renowned for spoiling people with their excess at their official parties. He has not been back since.

I reasoned that in applying for the job of Scilly Sergeant, I was not necessarily going to be up against a wall of other hopefuls; nevertheless, it seemed unwise to advertise the fact, or to get other officers enthusiastic about the job. I kept my application quiet.

There is a knowing bond between constables and sergeants who have survived the Scilly secondment. We have been through the same mill and have come out of it changed, with unspoken mutual respect for having survived the archipelago. However, the bond does not imply that everyone comes away with similar memories or similar levels of affection. The posting can be a marriage-breaker or can sever ties with family members. My first stint of two years on St Mary's had left me with a sense of nostalgia, but this was different from the impression it left on a colleague of mine. A fellow sergeant I knew, who had himself been a Police Constable on Scilly in the early 2000s, bumped into me in the corridor at work one morning. He had perhaps not enjoyed his two years as emphatically as I had done. Our meeting that morning occurred literally seconds after I had put my application for the sergeant's post on the inspector's desk, for his consideration. Walking back to my office, I bumped into the former Scilly constable.

'Weh-hey, Col! Have you seen? They are advertising again for the post of Sergeant for Scilly. What sucker would do that?'

'Err, dunno, Geordie. What sucker indeed!'

I didn't bother telling him at that point that my application was awaiting the inspector's attention.

Just over a month later I was invited for interview. I was the only applicant who had stuck it out to interview day. I am sure I could have blown that interview if I had really tried but as candidate number one of one I somehow did sufficiently well for the post not to be re-advertised. I was told to go to Clothing Stores and draw a uniform to take with me to Scilly. I would have to ditch the suit, as I wouldn't be needing it for two or three years.

I think it is fair to say that I was eager to get the family to Scilly. It took twenty-four days from being given confirmation of the post to us getting on the ferry at Penzance. It was 24th August 2011 when we walked the gangplank onto the large white ferry for our second posting out to the isles.

ARE WE NEARLY THERE YET?

'Dad, are we nearly there yet?'

'Not quite yet, Lewis. Look, can you see that land on the horizon? That's where we are going.'

I suppose, for children who have always lived in a small village on Dartmoor, the idea of moving away from their land-locked rural home high up on a moor to one where the sea and the tides are everything was always going to involve a shift in their thinking. My children, Lewis (nine) and Isabella (or Bella, seven), were growing up to learn about the world in terms of lambing, fields and car journeys. Our family house was in a small village where we had lived in total for fifteen years, either side of our postings to Scilly – a commuter village for Exeter, with a population of fewer than 500. Like almost everyone's in the village, our garden backed onto fields, and our neighbours were farmers who frequently brought their work home with them. Neither of our children had ever lived anywhere else, and they had schooled in the neighbouring village. Their horizons were not distant, frequently being confined to high-hedged Devon lanes or the brow of the next hill. They rarely ventured far from me or Sarah.

Bella had taken enthusiastically to assisting with the neighbour's sheep. From the age of four she was frequently off in some corner of a north Dartmoor field, with Sammy the Shetland sheepdog, rounding up and feeding the pregnant ewes. She was an enthusiastic dab hand at lambing time, too, and for several seasons innocently jabbered on at dinner time with gory talk of breech births, dagging (removing maggots from the bottoms of sheep) or vaginal prolapse. And all this while tucking into a roast dinner that included slices of an animal she had named and bottle-fed only a year earlier. Not normal talk for most youngsters perhaps, but arguably a healthy outlook on life, and one that gave Sarah and me reassurance that Bella would be game for an adventure. Lewis was no different. He was busy learning to ride horses and quad bikes, and shooting tin cans off fence posts at a friend's field.

We knew almost everyone in the village – if not by name, then by sight – and they us. People were aware that I was a policeman, but my beat did not cover the area of the village, so I never patrolled or enforced the law there. I did not bring my work home with me, and my neighbours did not trouble me with their policing concerns. I made a point of not wearing my uniform to and from work, to preserve the distance between me and what some people consider my alter ego. The village was a haven from work, with little crime or disorder. I once caught a burglar casing the village, and recognised him from briefings at Exeter police station; it was a simple matter to see him off the parish before he made ill-gotten gains, and he never came back. That was pretty much the sum total of the moments when I put myself on-duty while at home.

So many things would be different on Scilly. For the children, their new outlook would be one of fishing, quays and boating, but I harboured no expectations that they would be any wiser about the world they were entering, in the time it took to complete our journey to the islands.

To start with, they had only ever been on a boat once before – an open wooden boat that we chartered with a skipper, to catch mackerel as a family in Looe Bay earlier that summer. This was a taster for them, and neither child was put off when the deck filled with mackerel splashing their crimson blood all over their clothes.

The *Scillonian III* heading from Penzance along the southern coastline of West Cornwall was kind to us on the journey out. We passed in turn Newlyn, Mousehole, Lamorna and of course Land's End, before leaving the mainland behind us to the east. We were heading west. This was an adventure and we felt like pilgrims, leaving our home, friends and family to seek fortune over the seas. From the height of the deck it was just possible, with an adult eye, to make out the shape of the islands on the horizon. Trying to point this out to an excited nine-year-old was nigh on impossible.

It helped that, when we most needed it, that first sailing for my family out to the islands, eleven years after I had left there as Constable, was perfect. The gentle up-and-down pitch of the vessel was dramatically offset by the occasional judder of the bulkheads, as the bow slammed into the oncoming rolling groundswell of the Atlantic. It is often stated that the sailing out to Scilly is rougher than the journey on the way back. This is because steaming westwards goes against the swell, while returning eastwards back to the mainland goes with the waves. The ship has a shallow draught, so it can use the relatively shallow ports of Penzance and St Mary's, but the *Scillonian* moves differently on the way out from on the way back. Most concede that the latter is more agreeable.

If I think the crossing may be rough, then I – like many seasoned travellers – scurry down to the lowest deck, to lie on the padded bench seats in what feels like the bilges and sleep the journey off. The alternative is to sit up on deck, facing the bracing wind, and stay cold, staring out at the horizon. You can fool your stomach that you are not in motion by looking at a distant fixed point, while edging towards hypothermia or simply becoming comatose under a blanket. These are the best ways for the delicate landlubber to travel by ship, in my view.

Others sit inside, getting all hot and staring at their navels, feeling sorry for themselves while listening to and smelling the anxiety of others who are doing the same. The ship has a reputation (badly earned, in my view) of being gastronomically upsetting. The *Vomit Comet* or *Sicklonian* are her unkind nicknames. But what some people consider a punishing journey has only ever been generous to me. I'd travel on the boat every trip, if time were not a factor.

It added a touch of adventure to the proceedings that the first passage the children experienced was not too calm and not too rough. A Goldilocks crossing. The wind and waves were just right for the seabirds, too. For several decades I have watched them and, as an enthusiastic conservation volunteer, ringed these pelagic voyagers across several oceans, with great contentment. They have survived in this harsh ocean environment for millennia by conserving their energy through effortless flight. If it is too calm, they struggle to find enough wind to give them lift, so they make their way with laboured flight. As the gusts go further up the Beaufort scale, the going gets easier for them. I tried to explain this to the children, but they just wanted to run about the deck. I took the opportunity to sit and watch the spectacle of shearwaters, gannets and fulmars flying alongside the ship – the gannets quartering the water from a height of ninety feet, and the shearwaters and fulmars lower down, skimming the waves, the primaries on their wing tips just millimetres from the surface. They were all expertly looking for the next uplift from the crest of a wave and chasing the same goal: the shoals of bait fish driven to the surface by larger mackerel.

For me, just watching these birds on the wing transported me back in time to my career as a conservation biologist, before swearing office as a police officer, aged twenty-eight. From the late 1980s to the mid-1990s I had a very different life, working on projects with birds around the world, from Shetland to the Seychelles, Mauritius and Madagascar and other remote places besides; managing populations of endangered birds and their habitats. I'm no twitcher and, if truth be told, I don't need to check off a list of new birds; just give me fulmars, gannets and shearwaters and I'll be content.

The Isles of Scilly Steamship Company runs the ferry and, for the interest of passengers, offers passage to a naturalist called Paul, from Penzance. Other than the crew, Paul must take more trips back and forth to Scilly than anyone else. He stands out on deck with his binoculars, come rain or shine, scanning the horizon for wildlife of interest to point out to passengers. He was on our voyage out and told me of previous sightings of breaching humpbacks, minke and beaked whales, as well as other species of seabirds. We saw none of these massive sea mammals on our sailing, but we did spot dolphins, porpoises and giant jellyfish. The journey by boat can be like a David Attenborough documentary and, for my money, the sail out to Scilly is as enjoyable as actually arriving.

Lewis and Bella ran around the deck of the ship for the first hour, excited to be out of the car, before exhausting their energy and collapsing to sleep on our laps. Sarah and I were happy just to sit and relax, feeling knackered after a hectic few days of packing up all our belongings. Our worldly goods were in crates that were now in the hold of the ship beneath us. The removal company was ahead of us, having travelled by air, and would be waiting at St Mary's for our containers. The cost of moving a family to these islands is more expensive than moving to Australia on the other side of the world. There are no removal companies permanently on Scilly, so the same team is used at every stage of loading and unloading. Our furniture and belongings were first loaded into containers on a lorry and driven to Penzance. There they were reloaded into a container that was suitable for the hold of the ship. Once on the quay at St Mary's, the container was then lifted onto a local flatbed trailer and taken to the house. The removals crew would be the same at both ends, with accommodation and travel costs included in the price. Our cat, Husky, was in a box at our feet. We were leaving our home on Dartmoor for at least two years and shipping ourselves – lock, stock and barrel – to Scilly. Again.

Two-and-a-bit hours after casting off, the ship had reached the Eastern Isles, the first land since Land's End. The boat takes one of two approaches to the islands. She either sails in a southerly swoop, with St Agnes on her port side and St Mary's to the north on her starboard; or on a northerly path through the Eastern Isles, past St Martin's and Tresco, with St Mary's to the south on her port. This depends on the state of the tide. When the tide is in, the water is deep enough for the northerly entrance; otherwise the boat has to stay in deep water until the last minute, just before coming into harbour. The tide was making (coming in) on our approach that day, so we sailed right through the middle of the group of islands, past the Innisidgen burial chamber and Halangy Down Iron Age village just below the golf course on St Mary's.

'Dad, are we nearly there yet?'

'Yes, Lewis, this is St Mary's.'

As the ship slowed, before pulling alongside the harbour, my son spotted a child only a few years older than him, sitting in a small boat heading out to sea from the harbour. The boy was perched at the stern of his punt, holding the tiller of the outboard and staring directly out to sea. He had a fishing rod and we could see there was a lobster pot in the bow of his boat. We watched him as he skilfully negotiated the wake that our much larger ship had left, before heading off towards the point we had come from. It was as natural to watch that child driving his boat in the open ocean as it would have been to have seen a similar-aged child riding a bike along a main road.

Lewis turned to me. 'Dad, can we get a boat?'

'Yes, we can, and by the time you leave here, I think you should be able to do that.'

I pointed after the boy, and together we watched him confidently make his way around the coast to catch a pollock with which to bait his lobster pot. I imagined that he was almost certainly born to the sea and was taught by his father, and by his father before him.

Lewis beamed from ear to ear.

THE COMMUTE

I have lived on Scilly in the same police house (with en-suite police station) along Garrison Lane longer than I have ever lived in any home in my fifty years – seven years, all told. Living above the shop.

There are precious few of these police houses now left around the country. I know of no others outside London. Certainly there are none in Devon and Cornwall. It is pretty much essential that housing is provided for this posting. Property prices on Scilly are close to the high prices in the south-east of England. A small two-bed flat will easily set you back more than £200,000. If accommodation were not provided as part of the deal, then moving here would be so prohibitively expensive that even the few people who are prepared to up-sticks and relocate would bow out of the running. Housing is the limiting factor for so many occupations and, as police, it is essential that it is provided here or there would be no takers for the job. Nurses, teachers, council officers and a whole host more are not so fortunate. So many dreams of moving to Scilly, to live the simple life, are dashed on the rocks of the estate agents, before they even reach the treacherous coastline here.

Upwards of 80,000 to 100,000 people visit Scilly every year. That sounds like a lot, but spread out over a long season from April to October, the hordes quickly get lost in the landscape and it is always possible to find a remote beach with nobody else on it. More people than that visit Truro Cathedral, I am told. Scilly still has an air of exclusivity about it – the place that is sort of overseas, but is not.

My wife and I, and latterly our children, have shared the three-bedroom flat with commanding rooftop views of Hugh Town in the 1990s and then again from 2011. There are three police houses, but as luck would have it, we got our old place back when we returned the second time. When we moved in, it still had the dreadful lime-green paint on the walls in the bedroom that Sarah had inflicted on us eleven years previously.

I am grateful to the people of Scilly for respecting our privacy. We do get callers at the front door from time to time, and their concerns are sometimes fielded by my wife or children, when they beat me to the door or when I am out. Mostly it is an enquiry about lost property, but every so often we get: 'Can you tell your dad that so-and-so is responsible for stealing fuel from boats'; or 'Here is a gun – can you give it to your husband?'; or 'We were delivering meals-on-wheels and can't get into the house. We think there is a body behind the door. Is Colin about?' My family have to be resilient, too. They are part of the deal out here.

Legend has it that nobody locks their doors on Scilly. This is not true in fact; it is a cosy myth. There may be a higher incidence of such casual disregard for security than in some urban places, but the reality is that most doors here have locks that are used, when the doors are closed. Burglary is rare. To my way of thinking, this is not because it is difficult to carry it out. It is because it is difficult to get away with it. My fear of this crime on Scilly is low.

At the risk of this turning into a lesson in criminal law, let me explain what a burglary is. Simply put, it is when somebody comes into your home uninvited and steals something. There are other burglary offences, but it is trespass with theft that right royally puts people's backs up. In my experience, the Dickensian notion of the waif and stray breaking in to 'steal a scrap of bread for the wee bairns' is colossally rare. Burglars are those folk who, by and large, need your possessions in order to feed a habit – be it drugs, alcohol, gambling or an unfathomable obsession for the latest cheap sportswear. To them, your possessions are only worth what they can sell them for, down the pub or amongst others of that unscrupulous ilk. A £10 baggie of smack (heroin) is all that is needed. Double this, for a moderate drugs habit, and you have a thief who needs to score your possessions to the value of £20 a day. These are not pawnbroker's valuations, either. They just want quick cash.

On Scilly this type of villainy would be problematic to make a career out of. The opportunity to realise a financial return on other people's property is pretty much zero, unless it is a wrecked ship of course. Walking into a pub here and attempting to sell the jewellery you have just stolen, back to the person you stole it from or their friends or relatives, is a tough sell. Any burglar with half a brain knows they need to get away from Scilly in order to profit from their ill-gotten gains. Most villains actually have more than half a brain, however, so they discount coming here in the first place. They leave escape by plane or boat to the logically impaired.

Some years ago there was a smash-and-grab at the Stone Shop along The Strand, where jewellery was displayed. Overnight a criminal mastermind broke the front window of the shop, reached in and grabbed a handful of jewels. He hot-footed it from the scene and made good his escape. In a city he could have vanished in an instant and sold on his booty in anonymity. On St Mary's he had to check in at the airport the next morning, where news of the blag had already spread. His getaway plan failed to account for the wait to be called for the flight safety briefing. The beads of sweat on his forehead as he checked in must have given away more than simply a fear of flying. On a gut feeling, the airport staff called us and as soon as we arrived, he knew the gaff was up. The jewellery was recovered from his baggage and, after a flurry of bureaucracy, he was given a room at Her Majesty's Pleasure.

My journey to work from home takes twenty-five seconds and the return journey, uphill, is longer, at thirty-five seconds. I walk, as it is a good way to keep fit. This minute a day of commuting adds up, I can tell you. Totting up seven years' worth of travel means that I have spent a tad over twenty-four hours just going from my home to work and back. Heaven help me if I ever have to travel further. What a waste of time! In reality, this simple forty-yard walk rarely takes just twenty-five or thirty-five seconds, because there are too many distractions and reasons to stop and take a break en route. I usually leave at least five or even ten minutes before the start of my shift, in case I get waylaid. The journey home can take the same amount of time, even at night.

During the day the journey-stoppers are more often than not someone who wants to exchange pleasantries at some point along the route. Betty Sylvester is our repeat offender in this regard – and long may that last; our sprightly neighbour, in her nineties, is often up and down the hill, back and forth to the Co-op or newsagent's. Always immaculately dressed in pink, she is a banker for a chat. And I have often found her surveying the box of second-hand CDs that PC Mat Crowe sells at the front of his house next door.

Mat flogs off his listened-to music from an old plastic crate at the end of his path. Passers-by stop and browse his stall for the tunes he no longer wants. He leaves out a glass jar, for the honest to pop £1 in, if they take a fancy to his music tastes. It subsidises his beer-drinking. Everyone is honest, it seems, as he is rarely down on his expected takings; and is sometimes up, when somebody has put in more than the asking price. Amazing what you can get for an old Black Lace or Steps album. This honesty-box arrangement serves to preserve the modesty of both Mat and the purchaser, when ownership changes hands for one of his more dubious tastes in music. I have to walk past this scene every day. I have seen people skulking off with the guilty pleasures of Genesis and Peter Gabriel. Prog rock – now what is that all about?

Mat's second-hand music emporium has clearly been to the approval of Betty. After a bit of encouragement from me, and chats about different musical genres, she has developed a fondness for Kasabian and Red Hot Chili Peppers. I hope to encourage her on to Queens of the Stone Age and Muse, when Mat tires of them.

Betty is such a regular feature to us that when we recently had our Custody Suite revamped, I invited her to officially open the newly renovated cells. She gave a little speech in the stately fashion that only people of ninety-plus can do, and expressed the hope that we would never have cause to use them. Then she cut the 'Police: Do Not Cross' tape and announced the cells open.

My return journey home from the police station is uphill. After midnight I have to do it by echo-location, like a bat. The street lights go out automatically and if there is no moonlight it is, without a word of exaggeration, pitch-black. We have fabulous dark skies here. At no point on the 360-degree horizon is there any orange glow from the distant towns of Newlyn and Penzance around the headland of Land's End, forty miles away. The light from dim, distant stars is not burnt out. It is utterly impossible to see your hand in front of your face. It is as dark as dog's guts. I have to use a torch or the weak glimmer from my mobile phone to see that I stay on the pavement and don't bump into the wall or parked cars.

This makes for incredible star-gazing when it is cloudless. The Milky Way, the Plough, Polaris and Orion are in high definition. I have witnessed the faces of visiting city folk agog with wonder when they realise what has been in the sky above them all along, but has been denied to them by the stray light of their home cities. They don't lie face-down in the gutter here, if they drink one too many Betty Stogs. They lie face-up, marvelling at the swirling points of light, as if witnessing Van Gogh's *The Starry Night* for the first time.

The heavens are up there, and Scilly is a magical place from which to view them. To put the lack of stray light into perspective, there are times when the only light human beings have a hand in is the sun reflecting off the solar panels of the International Space Station (ISS) as it regularly passes overhead. It would be churlish to call this 'light pollution'. The sense of sight after dark is just for the stars and the meteor showers; it is of little use to assist me in my job.

When there is only the infinity of the universe to absorb, the ability to hear comes into its own. It is the time to stand outside and listen to the sound of the sea and the breeze. There is no industrial hum of road, rail track or factory. These do not exist on the islands. Just the white noise of the world, no different from how it was before the Industrial Revolution, and probably no different from how it was before human habitation. It is otherwise deathly silent at night after the last pub has closed.

When I am patrolling in the small hours near people's homes, I can hear the happy sound of snoring. Away from houses, the man-made silence is absolute. It acts like a vacuum, sucking every decibel of noise out of your body through your ears, and on a windless night I can actually hear my heartbeat. The silence is occasionally pierced by the infrequent, distant toll of the Spanish Ledge bell that sounds across Hugh Town. This is in a large cardinal buoy anchored a mile out to sea off Porthcressa beach. The swell rocks it backwards and forwards and the four brass arms randomly chime against the bell at its heart, to ward ships off the reef that it is named after. The still night air helps me listen out for any sign of activity in town. Countless police officers have done the same before me and will do the same after I have left. We don't talk about it. It is not in our briefings, because it is patently obvious to the late-shift officer that this is what they need to do. It is not an altruistic act. It is self-serving. No police officer wants to go to bed with the prospect of Plymouth Control ringing, just after slipping into a peaceful sleep.

The late-shift officer listens out for signs of trouble that need dealing with. We ask ourselves, 'Is that "whooping" in the street good-humoured or does it have the tinge of aggression that warns of trouble ahead?' Of the sound of steel barrels being dragged across tarmac and clanged together, 'Is that just the staff at the Atlantic Inn putting out the empty beer kegs for collection in the morning, or could it be drunken idiots pratting around, lining the casks across the road?' Of the revving car in the distance, 'Is that the last taxi or a drunk driver?' We are alert, assessing for good or bad sounds. Subtle nuances that give away what might be going on. Sounds that let us know whether it is OK, or not, to go to bed. Even when lying in bed, I listen out for happy sounds before being able to drop off.

If the Spanish Ledge bell is the only unnatural sound I can hear for five or ten minutes, then it is a fairly safe bet that I have put the town to bed for the night.

DOING BIRD

Having a police station as part of my home means that we always have two spare rooms. Lurking at the back of the station on the ground floor are the two detention cells, cradled securely in the centre of the building. They are made up, ready to receive somebody who may be insistent on staying with us for a few hours. These two austere rooms each have the luxury of an en-suite unbreakable, white ceramic, reinforced toilet pan, minus a hinged seat. There is nothing plush about the accommodation we have to offer. You know you are in trouble if you find yourself in here for a spell.

The beds are hard white resin slabs, cold as marble. In Cell 1 this resting platform is two feet off the ground, and in Cell 2 it is six inches off. The state of intoxication of the guest dictates how high off the ground they will sleep. The higher they appear to us when booking in, the lower they will sleep. It is safer that way. A thin blue, wipe-clean, PVC-covered foam mattress the same size as the slab goes a little way towards relieving the discomfort of lying down while contemplating your fate for a few hours. That and an unrippable blanket, for the well behaved, are the only soft furnishings.

The windows are rows of visually obscure thick glass blocks at head height. The light comes in, but there is no view out. There are no curtains, but that would be an irrelevance anyway, because a light is always left on when someone is in residence. A dim light for contemplative thought or restful calm, or full light for alertness and the business-minded. The walls are painted in Trade Jungle Green. This colour was chosen for one of two reasons, I suspect: either because it was the colour scientifically proven to induce a sense of calm acceptance and give the rooms a spa-treatment feel, or in reality, in these times of austerity, because it was discounted stock. The only occupant who seemed actively to seek out the cells to sleep in was Mowgli, the station cat. Nobody bothered him there.

Clearly the architect who designed the whole building harboured a deep-seated dislike of the police. Perhaps he had been fined for speeding on the way to work, on the very day he first put pen to paper back in the 1970s. If St Mary's police station was not designed on the back of a grudge, then it certainly arose out of a very special sense of humour. It was laid out so that the prisoner cells had party walls with the police-family flats, both to the side and above. Executing an escape plan that took its tips from *The Shawshank Redemption* would most certainly result in the prisoner tunnelling through into the neighbouring family's living room.

This was also one of those rare building projects when both architect and structural engineer were working with one vision. To enhance the acoustic effect of the inspirational party-walls idea, the engineer constructed the rest of the building out of sound-transmitting bricks, thus ensuring that all noise from the cells carries exceptionally well beyond the confines of the dungeons. The drunken snoring or irate profanities of prisoners are afforded Dolby-quality transmission to all residents living in the block. The revealing philosophies and musings of loud, disgruntled inmates at 2 a.m. provide thought-provoking discussions the following day around the breakfast table, for families with young children.

'Mummy, what's a wanker?'

'Just eat your Cheerios, darling. Daddy will explain it all when he gets up. He didn't get to bed until very late last night.'

For convenience, in each cell there is an intercom on the wall, which is within arm's reach while seated on the toilet. It patches the caller through to where I am the concierge at the custody desk – a full two yards away, as the crow flies. Amenities can both be requested and, indeed, demanded in some cases, at the press of a button. The first and most natural request for those seated in quiet contemplation on the loo is for toilet paper. Such luxuries are not provided in the cell itself, so they are handed through the hatch on a sheet-by-sheet basis. After bog roll, the next most asked-for necessity is a solicitor. The two things are rarely asked for in reverse order, but possibly arise out of a similar thought process. Every detainee has the right to consult a solicitor.

Long gone are the days of slinging a prisoner into a cell and leaving him or her there for hours, or days, on end. An arrest is often misunderstood. All too often it is considered to be the endgame – the punishment in itself: 'Just arrest them; that will teach them a lesson.'

Actually, it probably won't. It may put them off getting arrested again, if they make the mistake of letting Mat make them a cup of tea; but other than that, we do not aim to make the stay with us traumatic. I'd go so far as to claim that many people have positively enjoyed their stay with us. I know they have, because in the past we have had thank-you cards the next day from detainees. I'm still hopeful of a glowing review on TripAdvisor in due course.

An arrest may be necessary now and then to allow us to search a person or their address, or to compel them to be at the police station for an interview when it is doubtful they would turn up otherwise. On occasion we have to arrest, just to stop someone continuing with their unlawful behaviour or to better protect a victim; but, in many cases, we ask them to attend the police station voluntarily, at a time mutually convenient to all concerned. It is a much more civilised way to go about business where there is no threat of harm posed to anyone on the isles. There is no getting away from us, after all. We know almost everyone and, even when we don't, there is no real point in running away. Turn up at the airport or the quay, and our simple call ahead to the check-in desk will generally impede your progress off the island.

Infrequently, some people with warrants, for non-violent offences, like to tuck themselves away and Scilly can seem like the perfect place to do that. It is not really the perfect place. Not for those people with their noticeably anxious desire to go unnoticed. They tend to stick out like a sore thumb amongst the good people of the islands. Typically they will have a shelf life here due to the Walter Mitty lifestyle that travels hand in hand with their subterfuge. They end up circulating around a number of employers in rapid succession. Often showing their true colours right up to the point where their services are dispensed with. Then, their lack of purpose brings them to our attention. We make it our business to find out more about them. With their employment bridges burnt and sofa-surfing welcome worn out, they invariably come to the conclusion that their adventure on Scilly has run its course. It is time to head off east, at their own expense, into what they may think will be a bright new day. When the wheels of the undercarriage lift off the runway or the last securing rope is tossed aboard the ship by the stevedores, we radio ahead to our mainland colleagues as we wave goodbye to the deluded, misfit cargo. When they next hit dry land it will be into the enthusiastic arms of a West Cornwall police officer. 'Welcome to Cornwall, sir. Would you like to come with us?' is the greeting, and rhetorical question, that they are met with as their plane taxies to a stop at Land's End airport or their ship docks at Penzance quay.

Those wanted on warrant have to be presented before court within twenty-four hours. As we do not have a permanent court on Scilly this must be a court on the mainland, at Truro or Bodmin. Holding prisoners for any length of time on Scilly is not a viable option. Were we to arrest a wanted person at short notice, two of us from here would have to act as escorts back to Cornwall, thus leaving only one full-time colleague and our one Special Constable, Tess Lloyd, which is considered to be below minimum resilience. We will do this if the circumstances necessitate that. The decision is primarily based on whether that person poses a risk to anyone on the islands. We also have to take into consideration that the pilot of any plane or captain of the ship will not take a disorderly prisoner no matter how well they are guarded. Our planning has to include measures to ensure everything is done to keep everyone calm and safe when we find ourselves in the prisoner export business.

I have personally escorted several people back. On one occasion I took a man with me on the first leg of our family holiday as it was expedient to do so. We sat together on the ferry crossing, the prisoner briefly making up the fifth member of the Taylor party. We were met off the boat by uniformed officers and parted company at Penzance as we had differing expectations of our bank holiday weekend. Mine did not include a trip in a police car and languishing in a cell at Camborne. His did not include eating his body weight in chips and chocolate in Bruges.

But mostly the action stays on the islands. 'Action' may be stretching it a bit, mind you. In seven years I have only had to run after a fleeing suspect three times.

Chasing villains is standard fare for a copper on the mainland. It can involve all sorts of crazy fun and rushing about, when somebody runs off. There is a buzz of excitement, as the event brightens up what might otherwise be an eventless shift. 'I've got a runner' is a call on the radio that sparks something in that ancient part of the brain known as the hypothalamus. Everyone and everything loves it – other colleagues, dogs, helicopters, and now even drones. Over here, if we get someone hot-footing it away from us, there is absolutely no merit in barking into the radio, 'I've got a runner. Can I have other units to Old Town' – or wherever. There is a fair chance the culprit would turn up the next day. Although we do a yearly pass-or-fail fitness test, it is rare that we have to resort to breaking into a sweat. The eight miles of road on St Mary's are not linear. It is a circular track. If the quarry runs one way, we run the other and bump into them coming back on themselves. It's like a villainous Hadron Collider.

The arrest is not the punishment – nor should it be considered to be so. It is very often one of the first things that happen in an investigation. The way we are to treat prisoners in the UK is meticulously prescribed by law, and breaches of it are very serious matters. At best, a denial of a right will see a case fail at court; at worst, it will see police officers facing prosecution and imprisonment themselves. It is just not worth a career, an income or your liberty to deny someone their rights. The Police and Criminal Evidence Act (PACE) was brought into being in 1984. It prescribes in detail how we are to treat prisoners in police custody, and how we can gather evidence by searching or questioning. This huge piece of law is treated very seriously by us, and we are tested on it regularly. It is our bread and butter. It is also a fairly dull read, in a thick tome devoid of pictures.

We do not make that many arrests on Scilly. Perhaps sixteen to twenty a year. One of the prisoner's fundamental rights is to be permitted to read the book without pictures. We keep an up-to-date copy just for this purpose. When offered, it is sometimes snatched indignantly, as if it will instantly support an assertion of 'I'll find something in here you are doing wrong, you mark my words.' Half an hour later the soporific effects of this dry text will have taken effect. PACE then doubles up as a shield for the prisoner to put over his or her face to block out the stark bright ceiling light in the cell, while they sleep off their intoxication. We take pride at St Mary's police station – as indeed I have observed my colleagues on the mainland do – in the treatment of prisoners with dignity and respect. I'm only going to bump into them the next day in the Co-op, after all. Why be anything less than polite and neighbourly?

Next comes the exciting bit. Everyone has the right to consult a solicitor. This is a service that comes as standard at every custody centre in the UK. It is one of the basic rights prescribed by law. Again, this is where too much TV is sometimes a barrier to a full understanding of the word 'consult'. Most take it to mean 'speak with, in person'. This is a reality for anyone on the mainland, but not here on Scilly. We have no solicitors here. At least not ones practising criminal law. Were it possible to provide such legal representation, then it would of course be our obligation and our pleasure.

Detainees who assert, 'I demand to see a solicitor now, and I'm not moving from this spot until I get one' will guarantee themselves a long wait. At best, and with good weather for flying, they will see their brief the next day, if the solicitor can get a flight; but usually it is a week or two later. When we reach this impasse, we invoke the wider meaning of the word 'consult' and let them speak to a solicitor on the phone. What often follows these calls is a period of bail, while we wait for both suspect and solicitor to be on St Mary's at the same time. It is still a free service to, them, despite the solicitor having to fly in from West Cornwall, and this slows down the whole process of investigation. There are few swift resolutions in many circumstances, and this can be difficult to explain to victims and the wider community. But having a solicitor does not imply guilt. Very often it is a prudent measure, even when there may prove to be no case to answer. We cannot guide the detainee, however, so the question 'Do you think I need a solicitor?' is met with stony silence from us.

Ours is what's called a 'non-designated' station. This means that we cannot hold people for longer than a total of six hours. This has something to do with our inability to provide round-the-clock supervision of detainees. Every time we have someone in custody, we need to have two people on-duty in the station to ensure their safety, and to get on with the investigation so that they can be released expeditiously. Long gone are the days when someone is locked up on a Friday night and dealt with on a Monday morning. Holding for six hours or less means that we don't have to provide meals for prisoners, but my wife still gets unaccountably excited at the prospect of feeding suspects, if their detention runs through the night into early-morning breakfast. If I am overly late for dinner because we have a guest in the cells, Sarah brings my food down to me at the station. She happily plates up a second meal for the prisoner, too. It's all very civilised.

This is all very different from the mainland where for the most part the custody units can hold suspects for up to twenty-four hours and wives of custody sergeants are seldom present. Solicitors are on-tap and turn up within the hour rather than a flight away. There is no need to bail prisoners, simply to get a legal take on the matter from the Crown Prosecution Service, as most matters can be dealt with in the twenty-four hours the law provides. All our arrests, apart from the most serious offences, mean that we have to deal with the suspect in custody within the six-hour limit. Arrest someone at 9 p.m. and they have to be released by 3 a.m. at the latest. Barely enough time for them to sober up. A lot of strong coffee is drunk at our station. Coffee made by Mat, I hasten to add. Another good reason – if reason were needed – not to be found disorderly in the street.

Arrests are, quite frankly, a pain, so we resort to dealing with most of our suspects by inviting them voluntarily to the station for an interview. This means no booking them into custody, as they are not under arrest. Just interview them, then they go to their home in time for tea. They still get a free solicitor, but the risk of upsetting and evicting the cat simply to install a new tenant for a spot of 'cell therapy' behind the steel door is avoided.

The combined effect of all these complex considerations means that the cells don't get used much. For the most part, they define 'dormant' – 'as redundant as a detention cell on Scilly', you might say. This peace and quiet are what Mowgli likes. By the height of the summer, when the children have broken up for the vacation and everyone appears to be on holiday over here, occupancy rates on the island are at maximum capacity. Our cells are the only empty rooms. With a few minor adaptations, I could probably rent them out on Airbnb for a small fortune.

The door that seals the cells weighs 275 pounds. When it shuts, it does so with a 'clang!' that makes the whole building shake. The interior face of the door is featureless – there is no handle and no keyhole to look through. At chest height there is an eight-by-four-inch metal hatch that can be operated from the free side of the door. It feels very lonely in a cell when the door closes behind you, I can tell you.

The incident started with an assault on a minor, perpetrated by an offender named Rocky.

Rocky was one of our occasional station cats and an erstwhile prolific offender. The tiny black cat was the runt of her litter. She was found abandoned, hanging up on the branch of a tree somewhere in Cornwall, inside a plastic bag with her siblings. The litter was rescued and, through a series of fantastic journeys and families, Rocky found her way to our home on Scilly, where we adopted her. She wasn't much of a lap cat, being always alert and up for exploration. I have had several people tell me that she used to check up on our neighbours, crawling in to sleep on their beds with them at night, then back to us in the morning.

A curious kitten, Rocky used to pop into the station and check up on us there from time to time. In through an open window, across our paperwork on the desk, on to the cells for a drink from the toilets, and back out through the open front door of the police station – a whirlwind visit that rarely involved any meaningful interaction with us humans. And she was, like many cats, a very adept hunter.

One spring day PCSO Shirley Graham and I were busying ourselves at the station when there was a commotion in the front office. It sounded as if someone had bust into the station and was fighting on the carpet. From our seats in the report room we could see into this part of the station, but could not see over the front counter to the floor beyond. We jumped to our feet and hurried through to the source of the commotion. There was Rocky, chasing a fledgling song thrush around the room. The young bird was clearly panicked, and the feathers all over the floor suggested it was injured. It was holding its wings strongly beside its flanks, clearly fit and healthy. Its wing feathers had not yet fully developed and emerged from their sheaths, they were still in pin, so it was not yet able to fly properly.

The thrushes, blackbirds and sparrows all around the islands are unusually tame, especially on the 'off-islands'. The complete absence on Scilly of large predators like foxes and badgers means that these birds have adapted to be pretty chilled-out. In evolutionary terms, they have yet to play catch-up with the introduction of our domestic pets. They don't generally fly off when approached. Many of the birds are so tame they can even be fed by hand. At some outdoor cafés on the islands the sparrows are so numerous and uninhibited that they charmingly flash-mob visitors, in a squabble of excitement, for their sandwiches and cakes – the avian equivalent of carbohydrate-devouring piranhas. It is not difficult for cats to catch these birds, and it is a wonder there are any of them left here.

We chased the song thrush around the room and scooped it up safely out of harm's way, then scolded Rocky, who appeared hurt and aggrieved at the telling-off. In her tiny mind, she probably thought she was being the great provider. On all the occasions that she had been through the police station on her patrols, she had never seen us lunching on a feathered friend, so to her way of thinking, we must be rubbish at fending for ourselves. She would have to do it for us, so that we didn't starve. Now she was getting told off for doing the right thing. There's no pleasing some people! Rocky headed off to provide for someone more grateful.

We didn't know what to do with this bird. It was not bleeding, so should we put it back outside and let nature take its course? This route would mean that Rocky would inevitably be the bit of nature that saw to its fate. We could look to hunt down its parents, but there was no guarantee we would find them. Rocky had a large territory. We resolved to find another place, out of harm's way, for the thrush; somewhere it could learn to feed and could mature to fledging, without the risk of featuring as an hors d'oeuvre for a kitten. The timing of this was all very inconvenient, though. It was approaching midday on a weekday, and the *Scillonian* ferry was just about to arrive and disgorge its passengers. Both Shirley and I had planned to be on the quay to meet the ferry, as we like to.

It is something of a tradition that one of us meets the boat, when we can. It has been done for many decades. There are no great expectations of spotting a villain on a day-trip, but just in case anyone is in any doubt that the law applies on Scilly in broadly the same way as it does on the mainland, we stand near the end of the gangplank and smile at all the new faces. I like to amuse myself by picking on the most bewildered-looking and welcoming them to the Isle of Wight or Jersey, just to see the confusion on their faces, before they realise I have punked them and they break out in a grin.

We decided to defer our decision about our nestling

until after the boat had docked. There was no taking a garden bird down to the harbour, so we had to house it for the time being while we were away. I quickly foraged around outside and found a branch long enough to suit my hasty plan. The branch fitted across the span of Cell 2 perfectly. The little chap was the first inmate in this room for eighteen months. I left the room carefully, so as to keep the bird calm, and pushed the heavy door shut. The automatic mechanism of the bolts sprang the locks with a clang, sealing in the new prisoner. Shirley and I then left the station to see the boat in, and establish that all aboard were at the right destination and did not have burglars' heads on.

Half an hour later all the passengers had disembarked and Shirley and I were satisfied that they all passed muster. If any did escape our notice, they were well disguised in shorts and T-shirts, and had traded their shifty-eyed look for one of wide-eyed wonder at the sights that greeted them. Shirley told me that she was off on some errands, so I wandered back to the station to check up on our avian detainee.

Once there, I took off my stab-jacket and hat. It was a warm spring day and it was uncomfortable to be wearing that kit for too long. Placing it down on the floor in the report room, I went to check up on the song thrush. I pulled down the metal shutter on the hatchway in the door, to enable me to peer through. The branch was still in place, but the bird was nowhere to be seen. Perhaps it was in the toilet area. There is a tiny glass window that allows us to check this part of the cell; it has a hinged screen across it, as toilets are private places. They can also be mischievous places, where prisoners wishing to discard items they should not have may try to do so, down the toilet. I pushed aside the baffle and looked through. The song thrush was sitting on the toilet rim. It seemed fine.

I could hear my radio going in the next room, where it was attached to my stab-jacket. It was a call from Shirley. She had found a local person who had a covered chicken run in a field at Old Town and was offering to have the bird in the pen, until it was good to make its own way in the world. It sounded like a great plan. Shirley told me she still had tasks to do, but would be back at the station later in the afternoon.

I went back to the cell with a small bowl of water for the thrush. Checking that it was not going to make a bolt for freedom as soon as I opened the door, I turned the large key in the industrial-sized lock of the steel door as quietly as I could. The chunky sprung steel bolts unlocked with a purposeful thud, and the automatic-locking mechanism reset itself. Pulling the door back carefully, just sufficiently wide to let me enter, I slipped inside the cell and, using the open hatch to pull the door to, carefully shut it behind me. There is no handle on the inside of a prison-cell door; it is just a blank face, save for the hatch. As the door closed shut, the steel bolts sprang into action and clanged back into the metal frame of the door, holding it fast.

Fleetingly I was satisfied that I had got in, without letting the bird escape. This was a short-lived satisfaction as I realised that I, too, was now a prisoner in Cell 2. My radio was burbling away on my stab-jacket in the next room and there was no mobile signal on my phone. I had no way of contacting Shirley – the only other person from the police station on-duty that day. There was no purpose in shouting for help. I knew all other occupants in the block were out or at school. Nobody else would hear me. There was nothing I could do but wait for Shirley to come back later in the afternoon.

I lowered myself down to the six-inch-high shelf, and the song thrush and I sat there, looking at each other, both of us prisoners in a stark, featureless room. It gave me an insight into the misery of being incarcerated, and I felt what it must be like to sit incubating the nest while waiting for the other bird partner to arrive back.

The thrush seemed completely unfazed by this whole scenario. It hopped off the toilet pan and came and stood next to me on the mattress. The conversation was very one-sided for a couple of hours. Mostly me cursing my stupidity and figuring out what I was going to say to Shirley when she returned.

At about 4 p.m. I heard her come back into the police station. I went to the hatch. I knew that if I let on that I was trapped inside, she would most probably leave me there until she had: a) stopped laughing; and b) exacted the promise of an expensive forfeit for my stupidity. If I could just get her to open the door before she twigged, I could limit the damage to my ego.

So as casually as I could, I called out, 'Shirl, come and have a look at the bird.'

She came into the corridor outside the cells. 'Where are you?'

'I'm in Cell 2, with the little chap. Come on in, but be careful not to scare the bird when you open the door.'

She hadn't twigged that I was locked in. Standing back

from the door, I heard her turn the key on the lock and the bolts draw back, resetting themselves with a clunk. Tentatively she opened the door ajar and slipped in. She put her hand up to the hatch, as I had done, to pull it shut behind her.

'NOOOOOOOOOOO!'

Everything went into slow motion as I lurched across the cell to barge her out of the way and jam my foot between the door and the frame, before the bolts did their trick again. I made it. Turning to Shirley, I saw her face turn from shock at having been so roughly shoved aside to one of complete derision, as she realised I had been locked in all along.

Incarcerating myself had clearly been a doughnutable offence and I paid the price. I argued for a slightly reduced sentence, because of the fact that Shirley had all but fallen for the same error and nearly locked us both in. I limped for the rest of the day, too. One-eighth of a ton of security door crushing my foot against the door frame played havoc with my ability to proceed in a westerly direction.

We took the song thrush to the chicken run in Old Town, and a week later we were delighted to hear that the bird had fed well and had been fit enough to fend for itself. It had flown off and was seen briefly a week after that, near the chickens' home, suggesting to us that it was finding its way in life and surviving. I'm guessing it may even have had an advantage amongst the other wildlife. Presumably, with its time spent on remand in the cells at such a young age, it could present itself as pretty credible amongst the avian criminal fraternity. I have no doubt that by now it is the boss of a squadron of hardened thieving sparrows – a sort of Dickensian Fagin of the bird world, coordinating the larceny of the smaller birds; amassing stolen crumbs of Victoria sponge and chocolate brownies at cafes up country like Juliet's Garden restaurant or Carn Vean Café.

THE WEDDING THAT
WENT WITH A BANG

It seems intrusive and excitable to use the sirens on the police Land Rover in such a small, quiet place. They have only been used once, to my knowledge – and not by me, I hasten to add.

Once in a blue moon we have an officer from the mainland come over to supplement our ranks. Generally this is because our numbers are depleted through a clash with annual leave, for one of us, combined with unavoidable training or a court commitment on the mainland, for another of us. On more than one occasion, an injury has rendered one of us unable to work.

In the normal course of events there is no leaving the rock, with one of us already away. Two police officers on Scilly at all times are what we maintain, as our minimum resilience. There are very few planned exceptions to this rule. We have to be here, on- or off-duty, waiting in the wings to be called onstage at a whim, to play our role in unpredictable human dramas. The spare officer may be called upon at these rare times when the scene requires two, or the other officer forgets his lines. When there are three of us here, the third is essentially bomb-proof. They can do what they like and go where they like. There are precious few times when all three of us are called upon at any one time.

Days off, especially in the winter, cannot be taken back at home with the extended family and friends on a whim. There is no torturing the children with a trip to a National Trust property or popping to the DIY shop to spend money on a project that will lie dormant in the garage for years. For us, a change of scenery entails dragging the children to yet another Neolithic burial mound on the other side of the island.

There are more historical sites on Scilly than there are in the whole of Cornwall. It is as if the archaeology of the West Country was centrifuged and condensed at its extremity. People have been stuck out here on Scilly for more than 6,000 years. Alternatively, there is an inexhaustible opportunity for beachcombing – scouring the jumbled coastline for the flotsam and jetsam that have made the transatlantic crossing on the Gulf Stream, simply to drag the finds home, to lie dormant in the garage for years.

As the low earthen cliffs get eroded by the encroaching sea, it is possible to see the exposed middens, or rubbish dumps, of the original Scillonians from millennia ago. There is one at the southern end of Porthcressa beach, just below the allotments and easily accessible from the beach. These are long-forgotten pits containing mostly thousands of crumbling limpet shells. In effect, it is prehistoric fly-tipping of waste packaging from the bountiful supplies of the tough, rubbery-footed molluscs that cling to the rocks here – a remnant of a miserable dietary existence. But that's fast food for you, I guess; little changes, except that we now wrap the rubbery disc in something distantly related to a bread roll.

Sundays are when we feel at our most castaway on Scilly. There is generally no transport away from or to the archipelago on the day of rest. The airport is closed on Sundays to all but the rescue helicopter, which incidentally is the second-worst way to have to leave the island. Medical emergencies do occur, so the Cornwall Air Ambulance, the Navy at RNAS Culdrose and latterly Bristow Helicopters run emergency services for medevacs from Scilly to the Royal Cornwall Hospital (Treliske) in Truro, or further afield to Plymouth or Bristol if it involves a head injury or infant illness. We are well catered for by our medical team here, which includes three doctors, a hospital with nurses, ambulance crews and a health centre. Each island has its own co-responders and a tiny ambulance, sometimes not much bigger than a glorified quad bike.

The *Star of Life*, piloted only by one of two skippers, both called Martin, is the big, angular yellow vehicle that is our ambulance boat. Fall badly ill on St Agnes, and your transport to hospital will start with being stretchered on a quad bike to the quay. There you will be transferred to the boat and taken to the quay at St Mary's. The only conventional bit comes next, when you are driven in a normal ambulance to the airport, before being lifted off Scilly in a helicopter. It is an unorthodox and exciting journey, but not one that is enjoyed by the patient at the time of travelling. This is why it is the second-worst way of leaving Scilly. The worst way is being put on the *Scillonian III* or the *Gry Maritha* and being waved off in a box by Mr Alfie Trenear – Alfie being the undertaker.

Similarly, there is no ferry back and forth on a Sunday for all but ten weeks a year at the height of summer. Of course you could hire James Stedeford and *Tornado*, his jet boat, for the forty-mile trip, if your need is imperative. A few people do bring their own planes to St Mary's, or helicopters to Tresco. These are private trips, though, and not ones that we can capitalise on.

We had a visiting Police Constable, Tom, here a few years back. Standing in for a colleague on leave, he was kicking his heels and needed something to do, so I asked him to go and check on the Landy, to see if it was in order and that none of our kit was missing.

Diligently Tom set about our checksheet, making sure all the lights worked and the tyres were of the correct pressure and not worn. The rear of our Land Rover Defender holds a cage where we keep our emergency kit: things like signs and cones for the road, tabards, and tape to cordon areas, if we are called to manage a disaster. Tom dutifully ticked off each item to complete the inventory, confirming that everything was present and correct. Happy in the knowledge that he was getting on with something for half an hour, I left him in the street with the car and returned to the police station to do some contemplative report-writing. Five minutes later the peace and tranquillity of the early afternoon were shattered and I nearly jumped out of my skin. The two-tone sirens were sounding at full blast.

Not since wartime air raids had the sirens been sounded. People would be diving under their kitchen tables in panic. What was Tom doing? I had to stop him.

I rushed out to the front of the police station, to see the strobes going on the top of the Land Rover. Some tourists roaming past were in visible shock, looking around to try and identify where the threat was coming from. As I crossed the road towards the car, I could see Tom sitting in the driver's seat, marking off the vehicle checksheet on his clipboard. He turned the sirens and strobes off before I got to him, with a look of satisfied concentration on his face as he ticked the previously ignored 'sirens' box on the checksheet.

Let's face it, there is no part of St Mary's more than a ten-minute drive away from the start of the journey. Taking the Landy up to warp-speed, with blues and two-tones, is probably going to shave at best a few seconds off the arrival time. More likely it will slow me down, as confused motorists ahead of me panic and pull to a halt in front of me on the narrow roads. With only a few cars being driven on the road at any one time, there doesn't seem to be a compelling reason for playing our theme tune at full blast, racing to get wherever a call takes us. An extra consideration is that sounding the nee-nahs only serves to tell everyone that something is up. Speculation about what business we are up to then runs rife. 'Where were you off to then?' is a guaranteed opening gambit at the next casual chat in the street. The jungle drums beat to accompany the tune of the sirens and a piece of gossip is born. We don't need that, and those we are helping don't need that. Sirens can be heard all the way across St Mary's when the wind is in the right direction. I far prefer the silent approach, for it is so less brash.

I do use the flashing lights, however. These strobes are within the margins of excitability that I *am* prepared to entertain. A quick blip of the roof-mounted light-set adequately warns a slower motorist or meandering pedestrian. It is a fine line to tread, though. In a busy high street my hand has to hover over the off-switch to stop them as soon as I detect the onset of panic from a pedestrian or a car. The 'rabbit in the headlights' effect sets in all too quickly for some. I have seen people who have crossed the road safely and calmly go into a flat spin and turn and scurry back out into the road, for no discernible reason, when they have viewed a police car coming. There is no logic to it. Probably something to do with the hypothalamus and the flight-or-fight reaction. Whatever Darwinian force is at play, it is certainly an evolutionary trait that I have to ensure does not end a bloodline.

Even then, using the lights still feels a bit excessive, to the point of rudeness, especially when we are all so familiar with each other. Unfortunately nobody has yet invented a warning device for emergency-service vehicles for use in more benign beats, like ours – perhaps a siren that does a little embarrassed cough and sheepishly asks to be excused, while you pass politely at a slightly quicker pace than normal, and then expresses its thanks after passing. Fix some warm, slowly pulsing, pastel-coloured front-grille lights for a less stark effect and this would be just about acceptable.

The last time I used the strobes was in the moments after a bomb detonated. I'll explain.

The quay at St Mary's was being lengthened. This large construction project involved dredging the harbour at the end of the quay to make a deeper-water mooring. The silt scooped off the seabed was taken ashore and piled high on dry land at the Porthloo boat-park nearby. Over the weeks, increasing amounts of silt were dredged up and the spoil-heap became ever higher. Eventually it was so tall and wide that it blocked the view to the sea for many of the Porthloo residents living nearby.

This angered one of the home-owners so much that she took it upon herself to take a stand and put in a one-woman protest. One morning, just as work was resuming at the site, Patti Brooks, a guesthouse owner in her seventies, became our first eco-warrior. She left her house after break-fast, crossed the road and scrambled up onto the top of the muddy heap. There she stayed, standing with folded arms. She was thoroughly fed up that she and her guests could not see from her lounge window over the mound to the view of the sea beyond. Patti would not budge until she had seen the man in charge, to get him to lower it. All work was stopped at the site. The men in their orange jackets and hard hats who had been driving the diggers got out of their cabs and stood around, redundant, on the lower slopes, looking up while she stood like Edmund Hillary on the summit, looking down at them. The site supervisor was summoned. He arrived and realised that deciding to reduce the height of the spoil was going to mean spreading the pile over a larger area – a decision for a higher authority than he. While a more senior member of staff was hunted for, one of the workers took pity on Patti and thoughtfully brought her a chair to sit on and a blanket for her lap. Less

Hillary and more Britannia now, she sat defiantly atop the sludge, waiting for the manager of the site to turn up.

She sat for so long on the top of that pile that inevitably nature called. Such was the resourcefulness of this formidable lady that, seeing she was going to have to leave the heap to pop home to the lavatory, she negotiated with the bulldozer driver. She got him to agree to take her place, protesting on top of the pile, while she was powdering her nose. Fair play to him, he kept his part of the bargain. He sat in protest in the deckchair with the blanket until Patti returned, in effect protesting against himself about the heap he had made.

In due course a senior member of the site arrived and negotiations were held with Patti and the bulldozer driver. The decision was made to lower the spoil-heap. Satisfied that her demands were being met, Patti and the bulldozer driver folded up the chair and blanket and got down from the heap. She went back to get on with the day's work at her bed and breakfast, and he got back into the cabin of his JCB and set to work lowering the pile. Within an hour or so the top few feet of silt had been taken off, so that it represented a foothill rather than Everest. Patti, satisfied with the resolution, went back home to plan her next campaign or bake cakes, or both.

This was never going to be one of those complicated and drawn-out protests requiring ranks of police to manage it, so our services were not called upon. Had I been asked to attend, I might have urged Patti to come off the mound and protest in a safer location. The problem that she was unaware of was that the dredging was turning up all sorts of corroded explosives in the form of live ammunition. Every so often we would be phoned by one of the dredgers to come and collect another live .303 bullet. Evidently, back in time, an over-enthusiastic Second World War gunner had been stationed at the end of the quay with his Bren gun to protect Scilly from invasion. In his lethargy he must have stumbled over a box of live rounds and booted them into the water. He had probably been harmlessly taking pot-shots at mackerel to while away the monotony of his actionless war. Countless boats and ships had passed over them unknowingly for more than half a century. There the bullets had lain undisturbed, slowly sinking into the silt of the harbour for seventy years or so.

Then came the dredgers. With the sludge freshly scooped out and piled high at Porthloo boat-park, intermittent summer showers would occasionally wash clean one of the bullets sticking out of the pile of dredged silt drying there. Once exposed, the bullets would again live up to their brief of being slightly dangerous. The contractors would call us up to come and take them away. We took advice from our firearms expert in Exeter. He assured us that these small munitions were stable enough to handle, so we collected them and stored the little devils in our ammo tin at the station, for destruction at a later date. Our bored harbour gunner must have been very clumsy all those years back, because we amassed ten or so of these bullets over the course of a couple of months. The .303s were no real threat to the eco-warrior with the blanket over her knees, sitting atop them.

The clumsy gunner must have also had access to a much more powerful weapon on the quayside. For bigger fish, perhaps. The silt revealed a much larger piece of ordnance one morning and we were duly contacted. Shirley was dispatched to collect it.

The first I got to hear of the new find was when I came into the police station the next morning to find that Shirley had been called to collect another shell from Porthloo while I had been off-duty. The day started quite normally, as they all do, with a 'Good morning, Shirley. Coffee? What's on today?'

'Ooh, yes please. You haven't forgotten you have that wedding today? Twelve-fifteen at the Atlantic, to pick up Alistair, the groom, and get him to the church.'

A month or so previously we had been contacted by a police colleague from the Cheshire Constabulary who was coming to Scilly with his fiancée to get married. Alistair had a burning desire to be delivered to the church for his big moment in a police Land Rover – and who was I to deny him this? I had agreed, on the proviso that nothing more pressing was happening. And today was the day.

'Thanks. I hadn't forgotten. Did anything happen yesterday that I need to know about?'

'No, not much . . . Oh, I've picked up another live round from Porthloo.'

'Let's have a look,' I said.

Shirley delved into the property cupboard and handed me an A4 Manila envelope. It was heavy, and I could feel inside a cold cylindrical metal object about eight inches long and one-and-a-half inches in diameter. With growing concern, I opened the package and took out a flimsy Co-op carrier bag, containing what was clearly – even to my untrained eye – a live 40mm anti-aircraft shell. The brass casing was bent and split halfway, exposing the highly explosive and unstable cordite rods inside.

With a bit of logical thinking, it might have been pretty

obvious that the clumsy Bren-gun-toting soldier probably had access to other weapons at his posting on the end of the quay. He wasn't going to be very effective thwarting the advances of Hitler's military machine with just one small handheld machine gun. Evidently he must also have had the use of a Bofors anti-aircraft gun. Possibly fed up with targeting mackerel, and with a dearth of Luftwaffe raids, he had turned his attention to the larger pollock, with his even more over-spec method for catching them. Not that much would be left, if any fish were shot with a weapon intended to bring down a Heinkel bomber at 20,000 feet. He must have lost this missile over the side of the quay too, when he stumbled over some of the .303 rounds. It could also be speculated that had this thing detonated at the boat-park, it could have levelled the spoil-heap to an acceptable height without the need for Patti's efforts and those of the bulldozer driver.

It was at precisely this moment that I broke the world record for the onset of a tension headache. About 1.6 seconds, from opening the carrier bag to putting palm to forehead, if I recall correctly.

'WHAT THE FLAMING HELL IS THIS?'

'It's a shell from the silt dredged up from the harbour, Sarge. I collected it yesterday from the spoil-heap at Porthloo. You said to put them in the ammunition tin. It wouldn't fit.'

'It's a bloody BOMB! I'm holding a bloody bomb. It could blow up the whole police station. I meant you to collect the little .303 rounds, not unstable anti-aircraft mortars. How did it get here?'

'I went down to Porthloo and carried it the mile back through town in the Co-op plastic bag.'

'Through town? In a carrier bag?'

As an aside, and just in case you find yourself in a future bomb-transporting scenario, I have checked and found out that a basic five-pence Co-operative Store plastic bag is zero-rated for its ballistic abilities. Had the shell exploded, the bag would almost certainly have been unusable thereafter. They are not bags for life.

'What the hell did you bring it in here for? The shell case is split. It could explode. What are we going to do with it?'

'Oops! Shall we contact the Bomb Squad?'

'Yes. Like yesterday.'

I later found out that she had not actually known what was in the bag until it was safely back at the police station. It had been handed to her by one of the builders pre-wrapped.

Gingerly I put the explosive device down and we hurriedly looked up the number for Explosive Ordnance Disposal (EOD) – the Bomb Squad to you and me – with the Royal Navy based at Plymouth, exactly 100 miles away as the crow flies.

What would have improved my tension headache at this point would have been a lazy response from the slow-pulse guys at EOD, informing me that it would probably be all right to stick the device back in the plastic bag, and for them to come over in a fortnight or so to deal with it. Instead they rather keenly let me know that they were scrambling a Navy Sea King helicopter and were flying out to be with us a.s.a.p. – and that we were not to touch the shell. A wedding; and now a bomb. This was going to be a long day, and my temples throbbed visibly.

By 10.30 a.m. the chopper and its personnel had arrived at St Mary's airport. Shirley and I picked up three khaki-wearing EOD chaps and took them to the police station, to show them our growing collection of Second World War memorabilia. They handled them all rather more gingerly than we had. The chap in charge asked us to identify a place on the island where he could make them safe by controlled detonation. I was somewhat relieved he wasn't actually proposing to do it in the police station. It had only been decorated a couple of years previously and I wasn't sure how I would explain this to my inspector in Penzance.

Shirley and I thought about this problem for a while and settled on Deep Point. There is a small, scrappy beach around the other side of the island, with nobody living within a radius of a quarter of a mile. The area is bare of trees and tall vegetation, with just low purple heather and dark-green gorse and the odd large granite outcrop or boulder dotting the vista. There would be clear lines of sight, to assist in keeping an exclusion zone free of members of the public. The beach was in the valley between two hills, a less-than-picturesque seaside location, formerly used as a place where builders and scrappers dumped rubble and old cars. The boulder-and-sand beach is scattered with numerous bits of rusting metal vehicle frames, relics of pre-recycling years. It is also surrounded by low cliffs, which would project much of the blast out to sea in the direction of Cornwall, twenty-eight miles away on the horizon. Pretty much ideal for a small-scale detonation.

We drove the explosives experts to the beach and they agreed it would suit their purposes adequately. Clearly in their element now, they dug trenches, filled sandbags, twisted wires, moulded plastic explosives into interesting shapes and pressed detonators into them. Shirley and I were asked to put in place a 200-yard cordon around the area – no small feat for just two people. This is where the long arm of the law was needed. We took up positions on opposite sides of the facing hills, to give us the ability to shuttle back and forth to the various coastal paths that lead past the beach. Coastal walkers were intercepted and advised to stand back. They all congregated on high land, craning their necks from vantage points that were distant from the beach. With the exclusion zone set, I looked at my watch. Time had ticked on. The slow, methodical approach of the Navy could have been a bit more gung-ho, for my liking. It was 11.59. Only sixteen minutes until I had to collect Alistair from town, a ten-minute drive away. It was all getting mighty tight, if they didn't blow this thing up soon.

Perhaps I had better make a call to the Atlantic Hotel, next to the Inn, and ask them to get Alistair a taxi. Yes, that was prudent. After all, I had told him I could only do this if there were no other pressing matters to hand – and an unexploded bomb rated as one of those, by any standards. He'd understand, being a copper himself. I switched on my phone. No signal. We were in a black spot at the back of the island, out of line of sight of the telegraph mast that services the whole of Scilly. I waved the phone above my head, moved to higher ground, stood on one leg with my arm outstretched, posing like Eros, and generally did all the things I could think of to encourage a glimmer of communication to show up on the screen. It stayed blank. Time was running away with me and I could now see that the EOD men were clearly having problems with their remote-detonation device. They were having to go back to the beach to lay a line of cable all the way from the explosion site to their safe place behind a rock, several hundred yards away.

It struck me that this was a perverse take on the familiar action-thriller moment, when the clock is counting down on the bomb and it is imperative it is stopped. I needed exactly the opposite. My clock was ticking down on a wedding, and if the bomb did not blow up soon, all would be lost. Long gone was my big-kid fascination with hearing a loud bang and seeing a large explosion. I had to get Alistair to his wedding.

Curiously my police radio was working fine, which was odd considering that it relays off the same mast as my mobile. I called Shirley and asked her to phone the Atlantic. She radioed me back moments later to tell me that she too had no mobile signal. Poor Alistair, he was completely oblivious to the prospect of being late for his own wedding, and there was no way I could contact him. He was probably nervously pinning a flower to his lapel and straightening his tie in his hotel room at that precise moment.

It was now 12.02 and my tension headache was at crisis point. To paraphrase Michael Caine, 'Blow the bloody bomb up!' was all I was thinking. I couldn't leave my post, because a small gathering of onlookers were with me and kept pressing forward to be closer to the blast zone, so that their pictures of the explosion could be the last they took of their holidays/lives. I had to remain, to persuade them repeatedly to stay back. A hundred yards away I could see the EOD guys twiddling with wires, connecting them to their manual detonator box. Even if they blew the thing up now, I would still have a 400-yard run from my hill to where the Land Rover was parked, on the other side of the valley. Alistair was presumably just checking himself in the mirror one last time and brushing his shoulders, in that way that all grooms do needlessly.

12.04: the boss man of the Bomb Squad looked around to check that nobody was inside the cordon we were maintaining and blew his whistle. Shirley waved back at him from across the valley, as a sign that things were all clear where she was. He looked at me and I gave him a wave from fifty yards away, in a style that communicated: 'Just get on with it!' But he wasn't going to be hurried, and I knew that.

BOOM!

In different circumstances, I would have marvelled at the size and power of the bang. The blast shockwave hit us all like a thump to the chest, passing harmlessly right through all the onlookers in an instant. The sound resonated around the area and beyond, bouncing off the granite of the exposed headland. It would have been heard right across the island. Anyone hearing it would wonder what had happened. My plan was to reassure everyone the next day, via local radio. Bits of hessian sandbag and its contents, along with a plume of smoke, shot a clear 300 feet into the air and hung there, for what seemed an interminable age, before raining back to earth, safely clear of us rubberneckers. I could go now, surely. But no, the experts had to check the site was safe. They waved me back. I looked at my watch: 12.05. I would be late, even if I started now.

The EOD man meandered cautiously back to the

detonation site to give the all-clear. A hawk could not have watched him more closely – as soon as he so much as twitched a hand to signal the all-clear, I would be off. Usain Bolt was never this tense on his blocks.

There it was: the all-safe wave. I sprinted as best I could the half-mile to the Land Rover, collecting Shirley on the way. I paused to shout to the explosives men that I would be back to collect them in a short while. Running at speed across springy mounds of heather, wearing a heavy Kevlar stab-jacket with radios, handcuffs, buttons and pepper spray, is ungainly at best. By the time I reached the car I was pretty much out of breath, with just nine minutes to get to the groom, and a ten-minute drive at my normal stately pace.

We set off down the rough coastal track, joining the tarmac road at the Normandy corner. A mile further on, the road narrowed and I could see a local farmer heading towards us in his truck. This was going to be one of those moments to find a wide-enough passing spot and squeeze past at slow speed. As we closed on each other, he turned the nose of his truck slightly into my lane – a clear sign that he wanted me to pull up alongside him, stop and chat for a while. I really did not have time for this.

This was my moment for the blue lights. I hit the button that switched the strobes on, to indicate to the farmer that I really needed to get past and could not stop to chat. We passed at slow speed and I shouted to him, 'Sorry. Can't stop. Got to get into town quick!'

As we pulled off and picked up speed again, I heard him shout after me, 'What was that explosion?'

I realised that all he had seen was a policeman haring

away from the site of the bomb blast. With my lights flashing, and waving frantically at him to get out of the way, he can only have concluded that Armageddon had started on Scilly. For the record, I briefly considered going back and explaining myself there and then, but Alistair was my more pressing need. I switched the lights off, so as to avoid widespread panic, and drove at my normal nonchalant rate to create an air of calm. Let's face it: we were late now anyway. We arrived in town just two minutes behind schedule, to find the groom and his best man standing outside the Atlantic, staring at their watches in that 'Oh, shit!' way.

The wedding party bundled into the Land Rover and we set off for Old Town Church and Alistair's new life. He looked the part, and I saw no need to burden him with too much of my morning's excitement. We drove through town at a stately pace and arrived at the church behind time, but ahead of the bride, which was all that mattered. A few snaps from the wedding photographer to prove that Alistair had been transported in a police vehicle, a handshake and best wishes for the future, and we were off again. We still had to get the Bomb Squad back to the waiting Sea King and crew, who were presumably on their umpteenth coffee at the airport by now. This was just the mopping-up operation and my headache was receding now. We delivered the chaps back to their helicopter and it departed for the mainland, to await scrambling for another drama.

Shirley and I made it back in the police car to Old Town just in time to see the bride and groom leaving the church, having tied the knot. On the back of the slump that comes after an adrenaline rush, I shouldered my way through the crowd. I shook the groom's hand, like that of a friend I had been to hell and back with, then reached for my handcuffs and pretended to arrest him for wasting police time. The wedding photographer took a snap precisely at that moment, and their main wedding photo was pretty much a given. It got published on the Internet and went viral. The happy couple had interviews with the national papers and with TV channels in the USA.

So that is how I came to use the blue lights, for the first and last time, on Scilly. Furthermore, it was the first and last time I will ever be a taxi driver for a wedding. I am just not cut out for that level of stress. Thankfully, as yet, nothing so desperate has happened that has led me to resort to the siren.

RUST IN PEACE

Incredibly, there are around 1,200 vehicles on Scilly. One of my predecessors had a count done in 1999, which revealed that 650 vehicles were scattered amongst the five inhabited islands. I repeated this count in 2013 and it had doubled in the intervening time. The population of humans has not increased markedly, but quietly and stealthily the cars are breeding. Don't go thinking these are simply cars that have long corroded in the corner of a field somewhere. These are ones that the Driver and Vehicle Licensing Agency in Swansea has told me are actively being taxed and insured. That is a lot of cars, or perhaps a lot of forgotten direct debits. More than one car for every two people; four seats for every two bums.

Most of them are on St Mary's. Driven bonnet to bumper, they would conga for three-and-a-half miles: the whole circumference of our A3110; from the tea rooms near Pelistry anticlockwise past Borough Farm and the upper duck pond, along Pungies Lane back down Telegraph Hill, left at Partin Carn, to complete the route all the way back, for a slice of cake and a wee at Carn Vean Café.

'Pah! That's nothing – roadworks on the M4 can cause six-mile tailbacks. You should think yourselves lucky.'

Well, we are. With just eight miles of tarmac roads on St Mary's, you could be forgiven for thinking it must be constant gridlock here. But it isn't. The majority of cars are static, either redundant in a field of old flowers or parked by the side of the road, rusting in peace. A constant visual reminder to the owner that, if they lived on the mainland, they would have little option but to drive. Cars on Scilly are considered a modern necessity, without there actually being much need for them. Fuel is 30 per cent more expensive here, as the cost of importing it to Scilly adds an extra tariff. It is costly to fill up the tank and drive anywhere. This begs the question why so many of us run our own cars, on such small islands. Walking more often, cycling or taking taxis would be eminently more in keeping with island life.

Visitors often query our pointless obsession with cars, in such a small geographical area. I guess the residents of Scilly are not museum pieces. This is not a theme park. There is no masterplan, with secret huddles of elders dictating how the islanders must behave and show ourselves to the world, like a real-life version of *The Truman Show*. We own cars; they are owned because everyone else owns them, and there it stops. We don't worship them. I sense there is even a sort of guilt at owning a car here. If the necessity for a car is queried, the response often shows that a raw nerve has been twanged. Few people here love and cherish the family car as they do on the mainland. Sundays are not spent on the driveway, shampooing and waxing your vehicle. Cars are largely left to lay static claim to twelve square yards of kerbside Scilly. I know of cars that have not been moved for years – decades even.

Literally within a stone's throw of the police station there is a Mark I Ford Escort that will never move again, but is doing a sterling job of standing point-duty on a patch of island. The un-driven cars are like unrolled stones – they gather moss, literally. There is no car wash on the islands, so the proportion of vehicles sporting an ecosystem is above average for a rural location. The mild climate helps promote this flourishing (and occasionally mobile) ecology. The flora and fauna on my own vehicle include two forms of moss, a lichen and a species of dandelion, as well as several spiders that have been in residence for many, many months.

Some private cars that are still in use and legally sound proudly sport species of woody vegetation, such as small pittosporum shrubs and brambles, as well as all manner of grasses, from their door seals and wheel arches. I suppose I notice these things more than most, because my job is to look critically at a vehicle's condition while I am on patrol. The fact that a car is a contender for a Site of Special Scientific Interest does not in itself make it unroadworthy. I am able to distinguish between construction and use offences, and judge whether it has merit as a Chelsea Flower Show exhibit.

There is no obligatory yearly vehicle test. Yes, it is true: there is no MOT on Scilly. I kid you not. Apparently the reason is that there has to be a minimum of two MOT-approved garages. There is only one garage here, at Porthmellon, and consequently the legal necessity to have your vehicle checked annually does not apply on Scilly. I have a hunch that there is a local conspiracy to keep it that way. Nobody else dare start up a competing garage, for fear of invoking provisions under the Road Traffic Act 1956. And so, without the necessity for a yearly service, the state of our vehicles is not necessarily what would ideally be required. They are roadworthy for the most part, but the harsh, salty environment and high UV levels extract a toll from their bodywork.

To bridge this maintenance gap, we have been bringing over a Traffic police officer twice a year, to pore over the island's fleet with a critical eye. We fly him over for a week in spring and then again in autumn, and let him loose on the roads of St Mary's – a popular move by few standards. I am reliably informed that the dodgy cars get hidden; spirited away in fields and sheds for the duration of the presence of the white-hatted police officer, or 'Black Rat' as he is affectionately called in police parlance. There seems to be far less traffic on the roads at this time, with more people opting to leave their cars at home during these policing initiatives. There seems to be a renewed enthusiasm for walking, so our road-policing efforts have secondary health benefits, too – a win–win for everybody.

Generally the condition of the vehicles on Scilly is getting better, and fewer horrors are evident. Typically some tyres will be sporting slicks that would be the envy of the best Formula 1 drivers. Other cars are permanently in stealth- or motorbike-mode, with just one or no back-lights working. These are the things my novice beat-officer eye spots. The Traffic guys notice things like worn CV joints, rusted exhaust brackets, leaking brakes and empty squirty-liquid containers to wash the windscreen. I am reliably informed that the skilled Traffic eye can tell if a driver predominantly drives clockwise or anticlockwise around the island, depending on his car's tyre wear.

Travelling out to Scilly with the family on the Scillonian III after the adrenaline wore off.

The Scillonian III sailing into Scilly waters. Bryher and Tresco in background.

Lewis and Bella arriving on Scilly for the first time in 2011.

St Agnes and Gugh. The largest island in the world now free of rats to protect the nesting shearwaters.

West side of Tresco looking east with the channel between it and Bryher.

Hugh Town and St Mary's harbour looking out into the Atlantic. Next landfall Mrs Liddy's in Torbay, Newfoundland.

The busiest English police station south west of Lands End.

The IOSPD team in 2015 Shirley Graham, Nic Gould, Me, Tess Lloyd and Mat Crowe.

True action heroes. Emergency Services Pasty Champions 2011 Marc Blyth, Shirley Graham, Mat Collier.

Merryn Smith being heckled by Shirley as Inspector Jean Phillips presents his Long Service medal for being our Special Constable on Scilly for 10 years. Yes, he is also the man who checks you onto your flight at the airport.

Spanish Ledge Bell. When all I can hear is this tolling a mile out to sea the town has gone to bed.

Right: Each year the World Pilot Gig Championships are held on Scilly. Hundreds of crews converge on Scilly from all over the world to compete both at sea and later in the bar.

Prolific youth offender Rocky keeping tabs on the case against her.

Me with a touch of thrush.

As "reward" for switching on the sirens on the Police Land Rover I gave PC Tom a more taxing vehicle check. He got bored of that and arrested a Drink Driver instead.

Speed Gunning Cars. Caution: At 21kph a pimped up cardboard toilet tube on wheels can inflict wounds.

Every year we offer an amnesty to those vehicle owners who volunteer their car to us for a spot-check by our Traffic officers. Terms and conditions apply, and simply because this is in print does not imply that it will continue. At a moment's notice we may just go for gold and give up the softly-softly approach. The amnesty means that any irregularities can be dealt with by way of an official-looking bit of paper, listing the defects or plant-species that are apparent. We ask that the owner fixes or prunes those failings within a couple of weeks and, when this is done, presents their car to us at the police station for judging. We then kick the tyres and generally check and admire the regulation tyre-tread depth, operational headlights, clean windscreens and topiary efforts.

With respect, the off-island cars are a different game altogether. The cement or earth roads on St Martin's, Bryher and St Agnes are built and maintained by the Duchy of Cornwall. There are vehicles there that define 'rustic' to a tee. There is every colour, as long as it is iron oxide – perhaps not surprisingly, because these locations are harsher environments. The winter storms blow salt spray over everything. The flimsy sheet-metal of a modern car is no match for sodium chloride. Chassis rust through faster here than boiling water makes a hole in thin ice. The old stone houses are not built with garages, and even when there is a shed, it usually harbours a boat or far more cherished and useful possessions, like lobster pots. The off-islands are a quantum leap backwards in time, even from St Mary's. One of the striking things about returning to the mainland every so often is seeing clean, modern-styled cars everywhere. There seems to be no hunger for the flash status symbol where I police. Owning a brand-new car on these three islands would certainly buck the trend. Tresco is different again, running and maintaining its own fleet of road-legal golf buggies, and in this respect it is quite at odds with the other islands.

Nowadays, the really rusted and useless vehicles are taken to the mainland for scrap. They are first pillaged of their decent tyres, if there are any, and then taken down to the quay to await transport back to Penzance on the supply ship, the *Gry Maritha*. Up till fairly recent times, old cars (and even larger vehicles) were taken up to the top of the cliff at Deep Point on the eastern side of St Mary's. The cliff here plunges to water depths of 160–200 feet very close offshore, hence the name. The spectacle of trundling old wrecks off the cliff edge to Davy Jones' Locker is legendary.

Knocked out of gear and with the handbrake off, the cars would be pushed over the rock face, to splash in the water below. A local diver recently descended into the depths at Deep Point, expecting to see the remains of many cars. His exploration found nothing but a few engine casings from some of the larger vehicles. This caustic and turbulent environment soon sees to the complete destruction of the scrap. Whether this method of disposal was a specific criminal offence, I am unsure – it was fly-tipping, no doubt – but natural curiosity leads me to wish that I had witnessed it at least once back then.

Not every Deep Point burial went completely to plan, however. When the old council rubbish lorry finished its life by tombstoning from the cliff face, it forgot to sink. An air pocket in the large, cavernous crusher unit at the back of the lorry kept the truck afloat. It drifted, partially submerged, away from the islands for weeks. Covering many miles, it was carried by the currents out into the shipping lanes between Scilly and

Cornwall. There this large metal behemoth became a lurking hazard to cargo ships bound for Liverpool and Bristol. It bobbed just under the surface of the water, threatening to rip a hole in the hull of passing marine traffic. A complex insurance claim to file, no doubt: 'I was steaming full ahead at fifteen knots in my 6,000-tonne freight tanker, ten miles from land, in clear sea on a calm day, when a dustbin lorry jumped out in front of me.' The Royal Marines were duly dispatched to locate and blow up the lorry. I think that is what saw off the practice of burial at sea for the old-vehicle fleet.

People wishing to imagine the nostalgia of this environmentally questionable recycling need only visit the beach at Porth Minack, just around the corner from Old Town. It is testament to this former age. Amongst the large, rounded boulders and rock pools can be found the rusting engine casings, chassis and larger gear cogs of yesteryear. It is fascinating to visit. The tangle of car body-parts has been ground down smooth and turned red with rust by the heavy, pounding seas. Parts of the beach are practically made of metal – so much so that it is fun to try and make your way from one side to the other without touching sand or rock. I wonder how many of these carcasses are still being insured annually and counted as 'active' on the islands.

GRIDLOCK

Not all cars sit redundant in fields. In such a confined space, the presence of vehicles and their movement around us feels all the more intrusive. The roads on Scilly are not laid out for motorised traffic. Cambers and sight-lines are mostly all wrong. This is nobody's fault and does not tell of incompetence on the part of the Roads Department. These are lanes that were originally set out for horse-and-cart travelling at four or five miles per hour. Roads from a bygone era, when transporting carts of daffodils and narcissi from the fields down to the quay represented the widest loads.

In 2014 most of the roads on St Mary's were resurfaced. This was a huge and expensive undertaking, which largely went very smoothly for the policing team, despite the colossal capacity of the tarmac crews to inhale lager at the end of a hot day on the burning tar. The previous forty-year-old surface was scraped off, and new tarmac was laid down by contractors from Ireland. The roads are now as smooth as an ice rink. Consequently the previous ruts and bumps that used to slow down the traffic are no longer there to do that job, and speeds are increasing. More people have taken to riding push-bikes. A Sunday morning sees the same guys going round and round the island perhaps ten times before lunch. Clockwise is evidently becoming the established custom.

Some of the corners are sharp ninety-degree bends. The lanes have high hedges and are only one car wide in many places. Full competence with reverse gear is a must, to make it as a black-belt St Mary's driver. There are few passing places on our narrow roads, and someone generally has to back up to allow both cars to pass each other. The decision about who claims right of way is based less on legal priority and more on personality. For the sake of a peaceful life, seniority generally takes priority.

It's a sociological pursuit driving on our roads, and I think this may be why so many people here express disquiet about the golf buggies that are hired out to visitors. First of all, let me point out that they are only 'golf buggies' in name and appearance. They are in fact perfectly road-legal motor vehicles. They cannot simply be driven onto the nineteenth hole at our golf course. Their speed is limited to 12 m.p.h., and all rules of the road apply to them. For the most part these buggies are electric, so they are potentially more ecologically sound. To some people, however, just the sight of them infuriates them to distraction. There is no logic to this – I think it simply has something to do with the fact that they are being driven by drivers from the mainland, who are less versed in the etiquette here. These are people who are happy to potter along at sub-12 m.p.h. or to park up on a verge that we all generally ignore, so as to enjoy a view. Heaven forbid if a visitor parks on the yellow lines – or anywhere else for that matter.

Some nameless residents even set up a Facebook site to poke fun and 'tut' at these drivers; it contained pictures of various buggies parked at different beauty spots around the island, accompanied by a tirade of invective from those who followed the site. I casually glanced at it one day, and the only offence I could observe was the evident fact that whoever took the photos almost certainly did so while leaning out of their car window and snapping on their smartphone while driving. I had to have a word with one driver/photographer about this, who is now grumpy with me because he thought I was picking on him because he was picking on buggy-drivers. To a great extent he was right. Personally I would be happy to see everyone driving buggies. Our speeds would slow considerably and, if we all used buggies, the roads would be wide enough for two vehicles to pass, without the need for reverse gear. A social leveller that might tip the balance of power away from the generationally entitled.

It is possible, and legal, to take a full UK driving test on the island, having only ever driven on St Mary's. This has a similar farcical feel to it as the legendary driving tests of some of the developing countries, where only the crudest understanding of driving is required; accounts suggest that in some countries a licence may be obtained simply by pulling forward in first gear for ten yards. I'm not sure if that is strictly true or not, but for one elderly driver I know of here, even that would be a barrier to obtaining the correct documentation. Pedestrians scatter in all directions as he revs the engine to 8,000 r.p.m. before engaging first gear. His gearbox beyond second is in pristine condition, having never been used, and the needle on the speedo has never gone beyond 15 m.p.h.

The Scillonian driving test presumably covers the basics of starting, moving off, a hill start and a bit of reversing. There is no exposure to roundabouts, zebra crossings, traffic lights or dual carriageways. Familiarity with the full range of competencies that are present in the rest of the world is not possible if you have only driven on Scilly. If you pass your test here, tackling the M25 or Spaghetti Junction the next day would be a reality-check. I would suggest this is worth bearing in mind if your daily commute sees you behind a car sporting an 'SCY' number plate. Just to be safe, if you see a Scilly driver, allow them *three* chevrons on your way to work in the rush hour. Thankfully, most learners now opt for lessons in Cornwall, followed by a life-enhancing test on the mainland.

A driver I know, and whom I shall call Selina (for that is her name), proudly boasts that she took her test on Scilly and passed after just two weeks of lessons. Her schooling in driving had been assisted by her father, whom I shall call Clive (because that is his name). It was a while ago and their family car was a Hillman Minx whose lights rarely worked, but not so long ago that Selina appears to be more than twenty-four years old. Clive, being a skilled motorist, consequently relied disproportionately on hand-signals to indicate his intention to turn left or right at junctions when driving. Sitting in the back of her father's car, observing both his reticence to change a light bulb and his adeptness at hand-signals, Selina took this as the norm. On the day of her test she went to use the indicators. The examiner, looking to catch her out, asked her to drive as if her lights were broken and to show him how she would indicate a turn. Clearly in her comfort zone after years of her father's driving, Selina gave perfect hand-signals and passed the test seamlessly.

Competence at driving is, ultimately, a good thing. Not least because for the entire length of every road on Scilly the national speed limit of 60 m.p.h. exists. There are no 50, 40, 30 or 20 m.p.h. zones. It is 60 everywhere (or 100 k.p.h., if you prefer it in new money). This top speed is nigh-on impossible to achieve without a nitrox-fuelled dragster, of which the only ones that exist on Scilly are in dreams. There are very few stretches of road where it is possible to get into fourth gear, let alone floor the accelerator, for the full fast-and-furious experience.

It is therefore an exercise in futility to attempt to enforce speeding offences here. We do possess a speed-gun at the police station. A previous sergeant imported it to the islands, before I arrived. One of his officers, based here years ago, took it out on patrol one day and played in the traffic with it. Standing at the bottom of the hill at Porthmellon, he zapped cars for a while, eventually finding one that was ripping along at a princely 37 m.p.h. The national papers had a field day ridiculing his sterling efforts. I have used the device since then to measure speeds, but gave it up when several vehicles collided with me at about 13 m.p.h. Thankfully I wasn't injured, and the derisory laughter of onlookers shamed me into continuing to measure speeds without making an issue of it.

Perhaps it's best to point out at this stage that the vehicles I am referring to were ones made by the Year 7 science class, while learning about velocity. They were constructed from Lego, toilet rolls and rubber bands. I was using the speed gun at the request of the science teacher, to find the class winner (at the sports hall). That said, a hit from a Lego projectile at 21 k.p.h. doesn't half hurt. We have not used the speed-gun in anger on real roads since that date. If I were to use it as intended, I can only speculate on how the interaction between the motorist and me would work:

'Excuse me, sir. Did you know you were doing thirty-two miles an hour on a sixty-mile-per-hour road?'

'Yes, Officer, I did. Thank you for stopping me to let me know.'

'That's quite all right, sir. Have a good day.'

In practice on Scilly, where I know all the drivers and they know me, a more realistic encounter would play out like this:

'Excuse me, sir. Did you know you were doing thirty-two miles an hour on a sixty-mile-per-hour road?'

'Yes, Colin. Is there something I can help you with?'

'No not really, Ralph. Just trying out this speed-gun thingy, which has been kicking around in a cupboard for years. I hope you don't mind?'

'Not at all. Here, when is your next day off? Do you fancy helping me lift a few crab pots? I've got the Eastern Isles to do.'

'Yeah – Wednesday. How's that for you?'

'Winds coming in easterly then. Can you do Tuesday? Tides are better.'

'Tuesday's good. I'll be up at your place for eight-thirty.'

'Great. See you then. Glad you stopped me now.'

'Nice one. Drive carefully.'

'I was.'
'I know.'
'Bye.'

I have seen what constitutes a traffic jam here several times.
If witnessing the spectacle of traffic snarl-ups is your thing,
then the pinch-point outside Mumford's newsagents or at
the other end of the street outside the Atlantic Inn is the
best place to take up a spectator position. Such snarl-ups
rarely involve more than six cars and are generally the result
of some crass parking by a third party, causing a partial
blockage in the road, or of temporary roadworks. These
jams can last upwards of thirty seconds – a massive incon-
venience to everyone, and a dreaded traffic duty for us at
the police station. It is far easier to head such logjams off
at the pass, with a quick traffic bulletin on local radio and
the Internet, than have to attend and wave your arms about.
Following a call from my friends at Western Power one
morning I put out such a traffic bulletin, which, through
the medium of social media, managed to reach most
motorists:

By way of understatement, there will be some
moderate traffic disruption in town from this afternoon (Saturday) through to Sunday. Something
electrical and essential needs mending under the
road at about the Atlantic slipway. The road will be
closed to all traffic in both directions. It will not be
possible to go the whole length of Hugh Street. I'll
cone off outside the wide bit at Lloyds Bank, so that
we can all enjoy different drivers' interpretations of

three-point turns. The fun will start at about one p.m. and the event will finish in the afternoon of Sunday. No booking needed.

If you can't get seats at the Atlantic, there will also be a separate spectacle at Jerusalem Terrace, where there will be a diversion in place. For the duration of the road closure, this previously one-way narrow winding road with no passing places will be made two-way, allowing access to and from the quay. Be mindful that larger vehicles may be using this route in both directions. This will be guaranteed to test the mettle of the most reverse-adverse drivers.

Please do not make unnecessary journeys in your cars into town, as it will be a potentially frustrating process and there may be children present who can lip-read.

This message was well received and circulated, and there were no traffic jams on that occasion.

I have been called to deal with several gridlock incidents over the years, but one was perhaps more memorable than the others.

The sunniest side of the main drag through Hugh Town is outside the Co-op. It is along this stretch that I and my team like to bask and top up the tan, while on foot patrol. Like iguanas, we can soak up the sun, with the added bonus of monitoring all the comings and goings in the main street. It is lovely to stand there and pass the time of day with shoppers, but every so often it comes with the obligation to break into action and deal with something. And so it was that a shopper outside the store drew my attention to a developing scenario outside Lloyds Bank, a hundred yards down the road. I could see that several parked cars on either side of the road had caused a pinch-point outside the bank. There was no immediate and obvious concern for loss of life or complete economic collapse, so I took a relaxed view about the urgency to attend.

Police officers rushing to a scene miss so much information. It is better to saunter and soak up the atmosphere. I feel it gives off an air of calm competence, masking the weary dread at having to sort out two or more road-raging motorists. It is similar to when children fall down on gravel. Rush up to them and make a huge fuss, and tears are guaranteed, regardless of whether they have grazes on their palms. Mosey up, all relaxed, and express no drama and they may even get themselves up, dust themselves down and carry on without the need for treats like ice-cream and lollipops – and eventual adulthood obesity.

The same thing applies to motorists. Pitch up at their moment of angst, guns blazing, and the temperature rises for all concerned. This increases the chance of one or both parties demanding that punitive action be taken against the other, for some triviality that is best dealt with there and then in a cooperative manner, rather than four months later in an adversarial court setting.

And so I figured that I would proceed at an amble and the gridlock might sort itself out without intervention.

I made my way on foot to where there was a two-vehicle impasse: one small car heading towards the quay, and one large lorry heading away from it, with no way of passing each other. And a complete refusal from both drivers even to consider using reverse gear. With steely eyes and engines revving, both knew the other had the option of going for reverse gear, and both were holding the clutch in first gear, to take the advantage of the moment when the other driver capitulated and went for reverse. Not quite a spaghetti-western moment but, listening carefully, I swear I could hear Ennio Morricone scurrying for his tin-whistle and violins. No quarter was being given by either party, which amounted to the prospect of relative chaos in the scheme of things-Scilly.

The fully laden lorry, with its male driver clearly in possession of a sense of professional entitlement to the road, had been heading away from the quay before his path was blocked. He was nose-to-nose with a 1,000cc Mini being driven by an elderly woman with an endearing lack of perspective, who had been heading towards the quay. They were both static. Neither was sounding its horn. That is rarely done on the islands, for it is just too rude to contemplate. It is better to roll your eyes and huff, then post a damning diatribe on Facebook later, than beep your horn. Neither driver had any intention of backing down – it was a case of can't go round, can't go over, can't go under, can't go through; can't lose face. By all normal rules of the road, the Mini should have been the one to reverse.

The timing was perfect. It was the middle of the day on a weekday in June. The *Scillonian* ferry had just docked and disgorged all her starry-eyed, island-struck passengers, with their backpacks and their hunger. Most had not eaten since their sleeper-train buffet meal or their B&B's 'full English' at Penzance, where they stayed the night before. Grabbing a pasty at the café on the ship is no problem for the seasoned traveller, but those who travel infrequently by sea tend to take a nervous approach to dining while afloat – a caution that, in my view, is self-defeating. Think about being sick, and you will be. Carry on with your life regardless, and hey-presto! – the two-and-a-half-hour journey passes without problems. The beauty of a salted-caramel muffin and latte while watching gannets, shearwaters and dolphins from the deck is yours for the taking.

There is one type of passenger on embarkation, and two types after disembarking. All passengers board with pink faces and a strong, upright demeanour. On walking down the gangplank, a goodly proportion of them are still pink-faced, and for them the need to find a cashpoint and food at lunchtime is paramount. Then there are the green-faced passengers, who just want to find a cashpoint so that they can purchase a flight ticket for their eventual journey back, rather than take the boat. Some of these had already resolved never to sail again by the point in the journey where they passed the Minnack Theatre or Land's End. This resolution included the return journey from Scilly – a pointless worry, in my opinion, as the crossing back to Penzance is all downhill. The eastward-bound crossing mostly goes with the ground sea and prevailing wind, so it is much calmer than the outward-bound one.

The only cashpoint is at Lloyds Bank; and one of the first cafés, The Kavorna, is right next door. It seemed to me as if everybody, and everything, was aiming for this bottleneck.

It is a curious phenomenon that as soon as visitors step off the boat or plane onto the quay at St Mary's, they are immediately relieved of all responsibility for their own personal safety, or indeed for that of the more vulnerable people travelling with them. The previously heavily chaperoned child, who gets delivered to the school gates in the morning in Hampstead, is instantly feral. Children and the elderly are left to drift – almost aimlessly, but with the inevitability that, on such a small set of islands, probability will ensure that those in charge of them will see them at frequent intervals during the holiday, as their paths cross from time to time. As long as they all keep moving, they will surely come back upon themselves and arrive at the point where they started. That seems to be the general rule of thumb. And this place will probably be both the arrivals and departure point for the holiday, so there is no need to worry until departure time. The expectation is that they will all arrive and go home together; but what happens in between is a unique experience for each individual. People who, only the day before, had been navigating the London streets, white knuckles squeezing the blood from the hand of their heir-apparent, now become completely switched off from that parental responsibility.

Looking carefully at the faces of the new immigrants, I can read in their eyes the thought-processes that are occurring in the slowly acclimatising minds of the relaxed parents:

'Oh, look! A large lorry, with engine in gear, revving with a two-ton boat on the back. It's not moving. My four-year-old child is playing with the fluorescent tabs on the rear-wheel nuts. Meh! Where's the danger there? That will keep him amused for a while. We are on holiday on Scilly. Nothing ever happens here – nothing to worry about. Where is the cashpoint? Oh, there it is. I'll squeeze between this Mini and the lorry to join the queue.'

There is a perception that normal rules of physics do not

apply here. The 'Pauli exclusion principle', whereby two particles cannot occupy the same space at the same time, is an irrelevance. These are things for the real world, and certainly not worth bothering about on islands twenty-eight miles removed from that reality. Heavily laden solid trucks and small, squidgy humans are molecularly invisible to each other. Both are particle and wave-form simultaneously. Should they collide, they will continue on their journey unharmed. The street was thick with meandering visitors on a variety of random trajectories, all of whom were instantly immune to the physics of a collision with any of the frustrated motorists in their mobile metal boxes.

Despite my best efforts, I reached the vehicles before their drivers had resolved their differences amicably. I could see that other cars were approaching from either direction. They would inevitably nudge up behind the lorry and Mini, to form wedges in support of the moral position of the driver immediately in front of them. The meandering tourists were still trying to squeeze between the low chrome bumper of the Mini and the three-foot-high revving radiator grille of the Mercedes lorry. The child was still playing with the lorry wheel-nuts, and the parent was clearly not wishing to lose position in the cashpoint queue and deal with the dangerous activity of their offspring.

The impracticality of reversing a large flatbed lorry with an eighteen-foot boat on the back, through hundreds of randomly moving human targets of all ages and states of cognisance, was clear for all to see. However, it appeared to be of no concern to the Mini driver. The lorry might have right of way, as specified by the Highway Code, but she was applying the Scillonian rules of seniority and genealogy, and thus maintaining the stronger moral high ground, for reasons that dawned on me as I approached.

To the observer who was unfamiliar with Scilly, the solution was obvious. The Mini would have to give way. In this scenario, the driver could reverse while I waved her back and kept the undead roaming tourists from bouncing off her rear window. The Mini driver would of course object. A whole demographic of elderly drivers on the islands would thereafter label me as ageist. I might even be cold-shouldered at the charity shop on a Saturday morning for a couple of weeks.

It is moments like this that all seems lost and a confrontation seems inevitable. It is also at moments like this that a slow saunter up to the scene, and a little local knowledge on the part of the neighbourhood officer, is paramount. My decision: the lorry driver would have to move.

The reason was obvious: it was his aunt driving the Mini. In the game of vehicular 'Paper, Scissors, Stone', she was going to be the winner every time. I walked over to the lorry driver's cab and shouted up to him the inter-familial weakness of his predicament: 'That's your aunt, mate – your call.'

His shoulders dropped and he capitulated without protest. This was the face-saving solution he needed. Sunday lunches and Christmas would never be the same again if he did not relent; and in his head he knew it. His mum and her sister would make his life hell if he forced his aunt to retreat. He just didn't want me to have to point that out. My only other task was to get the child away from the interesting plastic tabs on the rear-wheel bolts of the six-ton truck before it reversed.

As he crunched his gears from first to reverse, the lorry driver looked at me with narrow eyes of resentment. It felt distinctly as if he were imagining the crunch being my nose, as his fist hit it. He backed the laden truck past the Atlantic Inn, while I herded the meandering green- and pink-faced visitors and their children out of the way. The aunt simply drove on past, at the widening of the Atlantic Inn slipway, looking aloof and without a wave of acknowledgement to either of us. A further twenty yards on, the road widened still further for her. She did a full U-turn, returning back on herself, and caught up with the rear of the lorry before her nephew could get up into second gear. Her only purpose in travelling into town in the first place had been to turn round. With this achieved, she took up position tailgating his bumper, as if chivvying her nephew along, to make a point. She followed him in his lorry down the road out of town.

I would have loved to have been a fly on the wall at their next family gathering.

THE PRIMROSE PRINCIPLE

Despite the idyllic ambience of Scilly, with the apparent air of an un-complex way of life, the islands do do bureaucracy. Naturally my colleagues and I do our earnest best to play our part in this, but by far the biggest burden goes to the council. We have our own local governance, infrastructure and elected representatives on the islands. No village-hall stuff, even though the place is no bigger than most parishes on the mainland. Our council is respon-sible for a wider range of amenities than even the likes of Birmingham City Council. Theirs is not to trivialise about setting up stalls at the summer fete and whether there will be parking on the upper field in June. The Council of the Isles of Scilly is the proper job. It employs in the region of 10 per cent of the working population – the biggest single employer by a long chalk.

The council has a chief executive and other officers. Every four years the community votes for elected repre-sentatives from amongst the worthies of the islands. There are no party politics in play, and the councillors are not bound by whips. Each has his or her own understanding of how to represent the community. It makes for interesting observation, as an outsider. There is a chairperson and twenty other elected members. Together they have responsibilities for a school, roads, sewage, water, an airport, housing, planning, waste and social services; indeed, almost everything that a normal council is responsible for – and more – with one notable exception: parking enforcement.

Almost uniquely for a council, it does not enforce the parking restrictions on Scilly. The modernity of deploying civil parking officers has not come to this place. There are no private clampers, and the islands have never seen a traffic warden. The glorious task of criminalising senior motorists is left to the three police officers who are stationed here. Even our own PCSO is unable to enforce the parking regulations. This makes us amongst the very last remaining police officers in the UK to have this dubious responsibility.

Contrary to most expectations, our thirst for ticketing cars for 'No waiting' does know boundaries. It is a dreary task, sticking little black-and-yellow-checked fixed-parking penalty pouches on the vehicles of your neighbours, who are popping into the Co-op for a few items. These are the people we live amongst. This task saps the last vestiges of congeniality from both officer and motorist. It is like a double humour-gland bypass. People who formerly came into the police station, just for a chat, now cross the road to the other side rather than risk having to exchange pleasantries. For a brief period some years back, I was even refused service at the Co-op when I gave a cherished customer a ticket.

It is all about aesthetics. Cars cluttering up the main road through town look terrible. Parking enforcement is the beautification of Hugh Street. I and my small team are its beauticians and manicurists: pushing back the encroaching cuticles at the side of the road; filing the rough edges while trying to make light chit-chat, before presenting a bill at the Nail Bar nobody intended to sit down at. Everyone wants handsome nails. Everyone wants a clear main street free of parked cars. It is the one road that everyone sees when they arrive on Scilly. Visitors who sail here on the ferry head up Hugh Street from the quay, to vanish amongst the self-catering accommodation and hotels around St Mary's. The ones who arrive by plane attack the same street from the opposite end, heading for the quay, to be distributed by small boats amongst the islands for their fortnight. Hugh Street is the main commercial drag through town, with the two banks, the only supermarket, pubs and a variety of smaller outlets and cafés dotted along its length.

Showing off this arterial route uncluttered is important. The people who run the businesses and services of Scilly demand that it is kept clear. The people who work in the tourist trade demand it is kept clear. The people who run the hauliers, landing all our cargo at the quayside and distributing our goods throughout our islands, demand it is kept clear. The people who rely on any of the above – which is all of us – demand it is kept clear. They all told the council, and the council deliberated: how could this be achieved? There was a debate. Ideas were put forward. The 'We must all just say No to parking' idealists were humoured briefly and outvoted. A suggestion to narrow the road with planted boxes of flowers, making it impractical to park, did not take root. Painting some lines and enforcing them was the only viable option, it was decided.

This was where bureaucracy really kicked in, with a debate on the colour of the lines. Yellow was too gaudy. This was a conservation area, after all, and the lines should represent that. Other colours of legally binding paint were researched and discussed. Beating a crisp champagne shade into second place was the acceptably named 'Primrose' scheme. A less-harsh, slightly creamy-yellow, to soften the visual blow. The task of laying down the lines was then passed to the council's Technical Services Department.

For many years, stark yellow lines were painted locally by hand in a variety of artistic genres, from abstract to allegorical, from *nouveau réalisme* to naïve art. All wonderful in their own right and much maligned, to my way of thinking, but in their own misinterpreted way unenforceable, by and large. Pointless yellow lines across junctions, of the wrong width (too fat or too thin, depending on what brush could be found at the council depot), wonky lines and painted-over gutter debris made the sentiment 'You only had one job' spring to mind. Irony and humour were all over the roads, if you knew where to look.

So the council decided to commission the painting of the primrose lines by a bona fide contractor. A professional line-painting company was employed from Ireland and the lines were competently laid down. The gauntlet was then handed to us, to enforce the sparkly new primrose lines from 9 a.m. to 6 p.m. every day of the year.

I did give the islanders a lot of warning about our impending enforcement – pieces in the paper, radio and social media. We considered a 'two strikes and you're out' policy, but dismissed it as unworkable. Would that be two strikes given by me and additionally two by each of the other officers, or two between us? Would a strike still be valid if it was given several years ago, by a different bobby? Just how would it work? I decided that the only workable way of doing this was to hold our breath and wade in. Day one of the enforcement came. The town was briefed; the lines were down; my book of tickets was ready. This was going to be a test of nerves. After many years of parking in Hugh Street, would drivers observe the new yellow lines? Would I really give out tickets? I honestly didn't know the answer to either question.

On the first morning of enforcement I booked on, kitted up and left the station shortly after 9 a.m. with what amounted to genuine dread. I walked down Garrison Lane to Hugh Street, where the unknown awaited. By this time in the morning the main road through town was usually chock-a-block with vehicles. Rounding the corner at Mumford's paper shop, I saw a clear road, devoid of cars for its full length. To my great relief, the lines appeared to be working. I turned to face away from the road to speak to a passer-by about this joyous development. As I did so, a golf buggy with a lone driver trundled past from the direction of Holgates Green. I saw it in my peripheral vision. My heart fell. I knew there could only be one reason for this driver, and this vehicle, to be making this journey. Turning to confirm my worst fears, I saw the buggy parked directly outside the store a hundred yards away. The driver was disembarking and going into the shop. This was make-or-break time: I had to confront my worst fears. I would much rather have had a large fight to deal with, or perhaps seen a shoplifter hot-footing it from a doorway. Anything other than this.

I resolved that if the driver finished his shopping and moved his car off the lines before I had reached him and put pen to paper, then he would get away scot-free. I could live with that level of discretion. I made my way unenthusiastically, with crestfallen resolve, to the white golf buggy. I got there first. With my notepad out, I wrote down the registration number and the details of the criminal offence, aware that my actions were now the only game in town for onlookers who had paused to watch developments. What would happen when the driver came out? Would there be a spectacle, with raised words and snatched pieces of paper?

The driver, an elderly man, came out of the Co-op and limped up beside me. A lovely old chap with an air of calm, and not a bad bone in his body.

'What's going on?'

'It's your buggy, sir. I know his first name, but the 'sir' seemed to give a comforting distance between our roles at that moment in time. 'You are on the primrose lines. It is past nine a.m.'

'I've got a bad leg.'

'Have you got a Blue Badge?'

'No. What are you going to do?'

'I'm reporting you for parking on the yellow lines.'

'All right, me old cock.'

With that, I wrote out and handed him his ticket. He took it without objection, clearly equally keen that we would both live to see a cordial relationship, as soon as this ordeal was over. To say I was relieved at his acceptance of it would be an understatement.

'What do I do now?'

'Well, I guess somebody will be in contact with you and send you a thirty-pound fine. If you pay it, then that's the end of it.'

'Oh! Tell 'ee what: if I pay the fine, you make sure you buys all your fishing weights off me in future. I make 'em out the back garden.'

I thought about this very clever bit of bartering. Here he was, taking the ticket in good humour, and all I had to agree to was to buy his wares so that he could make a profit to pay the fine.

'OK, it's a deal.'

And so it was. We both relaxed. He sells me good home-made lead weights, but at a premium over other outlets. We both lost and we both won. The first parking ticket would risk costing me more in one-ounce lead weights than it cost the driver to pay the fine. Enforcing the lines here was going to be an expensive pursuit for me, in more than one way.

Later that day I sent Shirley round to his house to help him complete an application for a Blue Badge, so that he could park on the lines with impunity thereafter. Rather that than risk another bartering that might be even more expensive for me.

So there you have it: the lines are down because the community wants them there. Aside from the tourists, the only people who can break these laws are the very people who insist that the lines are there. They still park on them, we still enforce them, fewer of them now speak to us and we now limit our time in Hugh Street as a consequence, but mostly I'm more cautious about how much fishing tackle I lose when catching pollock.

WEEDY GARY

The population on Scilly is not static. People come, people go. There is a group of big family names that date back hundreds of years, and it is almost inconceivable there will ever be a time on the islands without a Hicks, Badcock, Woodcock, Mumford, Pender, Dorian-Smith or several others. These and others like them are as much a part of Scilly now as the granite bedrock it is made of. Their family names are carved into the cenotaph and read out every year at Remembrance Day. At the other end of the scale, there are those who breeze in for relatively short periods: seasonal and temporary staff who seemingly wash up on our shores from all ports. These are the ones who find themselves on steep learning curves to fit in with the already-established social groups, cultures and customs. A successful existence in such a tight community is not easily achieved. Gangstas and the brash rather jar with the general vibe of the place.

The process of assimilation starts with bedding in and making a few friends. For the most part the newbie will be young, and more often than not the most likely place to strike up new acquaintances will be in the pubs. Most people do this with considerable success, as folk here are a friendly, sociable bunch. Every weekday night is a school night, other than Wednesday and Friday. In the spring and summer these evenings are turned over to ladies' and men's gig-racing and drinking. Gig-racing is not some sort of bizarre evening of competitive fast-paced live music; it is, in essence, rowing.

Conjure up an image of rowing in your mind from, say, the Olympics and you get a picture of a buff crew of Oxbridge graduates in Lycra pulling in perfect timing in sleek, delicate boats that slice through the water like razors. Pilot-gig rowing (as gig-racing is more accurately known) is as far from that as it is possible to get. Pilot-gigs are heavy, seagoing clinker-built wooden boats. They are built to enable a crew of six rowers and a cox to tough it out in ocean conditions, battling against swell and wind. Back in the era of sailing ships, Scilly was a port of call for ships from around the world. They would stop off here to take on board a pilot from the isles, who could navigate them into the likes of Bristol and Liverpool. The gigs were designed to enable their crew to get their pilot out first to the ships. First come, first served. The money that a pilot could make would feed his family and that of the crew. So even before the gigs were used for recreation, they were built to race each other. There is a trade-off between sturdiness and speed in the building of a gig. A heavy boat handles a stormy sea better than a light one, but a light gig cuts the water faster in the calm. Whether there is a perfect gig will probably be a source of discussion for as long as such vessels exist.

Ever eager to capitalise on any niche that presented itself, the Scillonian men of old soon realised that their own boats were so fast, and they were such strong rowers, that they could outpace the Customs boats: out to the ship with their pilot, back to shore with contraband of brandy and tobacco, outrunning the taxman in their boats. The Customs gigs got faster, so the pilot-gigs became even more match-fit. Some even rowed to France and back, to smuggle contraband, so I am told. So it is no surprise that the sport of gig-racing was born in the most organic of ways. Dare I suggest it: the birth of rowing races.

The crews too are as dissimilar from Pinsent and Redgrave in the Coxless Pair as the gigs are from their flimsy boat. Gig-racing is a sport that is done in woolly hats and wellington boots. These are tough, salt-hardened crews of men and women. The bare-armed rowers in vest tops all sport farmers' tans, have blisters on their palms and swear like troopers. And the male rowers are not much different, either. Before and after the race they carry colourful foam-padded cushions, made locally at Ratbags Canvas Shop, to protect their buttocks from getting blisters on the hard wooden seats of the gigs.

I'll be the first to admit that when I was involved in a couple of seasons of racing, I found it really hard going. This is tough stuff. Rowing anywhere is physically challenging, but pulling a heavy wooden boat weighing a half-ton against the prevailing wind and waves brings you as close to misery as it is possible to get in the sporting world. Everything about it hurts. I'm sure that the purists reading this will scoff, and point out that my two years of rowing were barely the start of an apprenticeship in this miserable endeavour, and I wouldn't disagree. Any sport that sees half the crew vomiting from exertion at the end of it gets my admiration. At this point I will add that, although I mock, I seriously admire those who row. They practise at sea in the evenings from the early spring right the way through the summer.

Each boat has a colour and a name, and their crews are fiercely defensive of their own gig. Followers of the gigs – locals and visitors alike – show similar fidelity. On the evenings that they race, the local ferrymen take tripper boats out, to motor alongside as the race takes place. Screaming crowds of passengers shout encouragement for their favourite crew. 'Come on, *Golden Eagle*', 'Go, *Islander*' or 'Pull harder, *Emma Louise*' is belted out at full volume by excited crowds. This is not a ceremony put on for onlookers, though. It is real. The line-up can include all the other St Mary's boats: *Nour-Nour*, *Serica* and *Tregarthen*. The oldest and heaviest boat, the green and white *Bonnet*, was built in 1830. There is heritage in these races. There are many boats to choose from and I have my suspicions that some new supporters simply shout for the boats they can confidently pronounce.

Support groups in their own craft from the off-islands converge on the races, too, and pre-lubricated passengers shout encouragement for the boats from St Agnes (*Lyonesse* and *Shah*), Tresco and Bryher (*Czar*, *Menavaur* and *Emperor*), and St Martin's (*Dolphin* and *Galatea*). Post-race, the crews seek refreshment and warmth in the pub.

A word of warning at this point. I sometimes use the pubs myself, when off-duty. Yes, just like a real person, I do occasionally zip on my human suit and pop out for a pint, standing shoulder-to-shoulder with other ordinary customers. To the recent immigrant, I am pretty much unrecognisable as a police officer – and long may that last. It sometimes serves to liven up evenings off-duty, especially in the pub on a Friday gig-night.

Some years back, on one such Friday night after the men's gig-racing, I was standing in a pub, pint in hand. It was very busy inside, shoulder-to-shoulder standing room only. It was my night off, and another colleague was on-duty. The general chat was about what boat did what in the race, and how the sea conditions favoured or hindered the different gigs. As always, there was a lot of mickey-taking between and within the crews. I had rowed bow in a gig called *Serica* that evening and fortunately the rest of the crew were facing aft, so they were unable to count the exact number of times I caught a crab. We had not won the race. I don't think any boat I was in ever did. For the 1999 season the eight-person *Serica* crew consisted of Kev Pender and Ray Brown, the landlords of The Bishop and Wolf and The Mermaid respectively; the bank manager, Mike Tonkin; me and Des Bird, another policeman; the Garrison campsite owner, Ted Moulson; Andy Hewlett from the Atlantic Hotel; and the cox, Alun Greenlaw, who was the only credible and experienced gig-rower in our crew. To Alun's chagrin, we were always the also-rans. In the 1999 World Gig Championships we came a credible sixty-third. Sixty-four crews took part. Alun stuck with us, though possibly because of a tactical advantage in having two pub landlords in the crew. We always got served first during the mêlée at the bar after the race.

The only people in the pub were locals, or seasoned seasonal staff. All apart from one, that is: a man in his mid-twenties, a pint more advanced than everyone else and definitely a new face. He was on his own, and nobody was paying much attention to him, as we were all absorbed in our own discussions. There was a lull in conversation – what felt like a respectful silence for a once-in-a-lifetime event – while everyone piled in their orders to Ted, who was offering to go to the bar. The new chap, who had sidled up to us, must have seen his opportunity to strike up a conversation and make friends. He muscled into our midst and turned to us.

'Hi, guys. You a crew then?'

I gave him credit for his pluck and replied, 'Yep, the *Serica*.'

His eyes focused on me at this point – I being the person who was standing closest and had answered his opening gambit. I was also the one closest in years and height to him. The others standing around were all six feet-plus tall.

'I'm Gary. I'm a new KP [kitchen porter] down the road.'

'Hi, Gary. I'm Colin.' I wasn't particularly interested, but I did not want to be rude, so I wasn't giving him any hooks for further topics of conversation. The others were not actively listening at this point, still waiting pensively for Ted, who was returning clutching several pints in his huge hands.

Gary was clearly intent on striking up new friendships. It was clear he didn't have a clue about my occupation, and that I had a warrant card in my back pocket.

'You from round here?' he went on.

'Yep, I live up the road.' Still uninterested. No hook.

'Fancy a smoke?'

'Sorry?'

'Yeah! Fancy a smoke? I've got some weed back at my room.'

All of a sudden he had my full, undivided attention. In my peripheral vision I could see that the others' ears had pricked up, too, and were now equally interested in where this topic of conversation was going.

'Go on.' I gave him a hook.

'I just got here. There's nowhere to get smoke on this island. I'm from Bristol. I've got some weed in my room.'

I'm no particular zealot when it comes to people carrying on their cannabis activities in the privacy of their own homes, but when my nose is rubbed in it, I have little option but to react. My crew were agog. This was indeed getting interesting. All banter about how Ted was unlikely to get another drink for the rest of the season stopped. I wasn't the bow-rower any longer to my crew. I was back in the mould of being the copper. My evening as a fellow human being was pretty much on course to be ruined. All thoughts were about how I was going to react to the new guy with the self-limiting shelf-life. I didn't have much option, but neither did I have much inclination really. I had had a pint and the last thing on my mind was putting myself on-duty for the sake of a bag of weed. I really wanted to recover from the race by spending a night off amongst friends. However, there was an expectation that I would do something. I had a fish on my line that had foul-hooked itself, and I was going to reel this one in. I figured it was one that could wait until the next day to be landed.

I responded to Gary, 'Oh, cool. Look, I'm with this lot right now, and Ted has just bought his first round ever, so

I have to celebrate that. Are you about tomorrow evening? I could pop round. Where are you living?'

'Yeah. Great! I could meet you here.'

'No. I don't like mixing weed and alcohol. I'll come to you. Are you round the back of Hugh Street?'

'Yes, that's right – staff digs: the ground-floor shed with the white door.'

'Nice one. I'll pop round at about six then.'

'Make it seven. I'm doing dishes up till then.'

'Great. Can I bring a mate? You're right: there isn't much weed about here, and he would be interested.'

'It's only a small room, but yeah, no problem.'

'See you then, then.'

'Bye.'

And that was the last conversation I ever had with Gary as a human being. He moved off, shouldering his way through the crowd, presumably pleased that he had skilfully made a new contact. He hadn't lost his touch. These island folk must be desperate to make friends.

Sure enough, the next day at 7 p.m. I popped round to his accommodation with my mate Des, the other policeman, and we introduced ourselves to Gary. He didn't recognise me in uniform at first. He actually accused my gig-self of grassing him up to my police-self. An indignant reaction that subsided when I took my hat off and he saw that we were one and the same. The look of recognition on his face, as the events of the night before replayed themselves in his mind, was comical to watch.

By the time Des and I had finished that evening, Gary had no weed left. We gave him a Caution for his troubles and popped all his stash in the 'For destruction' tin. News travelled fast in this small community, where many eyes were watching. Gary was pretty much a busted flush the moment he left the pub that first night. His employer didn't take kindly to the fact that he had drugs on the premises. Like most bosses on the island, then and now, he frowned upon any taint of criminal activity. In this instance, Gary's dish-washing services were dispensed with. He couldn't get another job on the islands for love or money, so shortly afterwards he left, bound for Bristol. As I say, Scilly doesn't suffer fools gladly. Gary's family name is unlikely to be featuring in the list of local names here in future generations.

TAKING A PUNT

When the founder of modern Scilly, Augustus Smith, came to live on the islands in 1837, he brought with him progressive ideas, like free education for all the children. From a young age they were schooled and the boys were taught navigation. Consequently Scilly became a net exporter of expert sailors. Young Scillonians were piloting boats all around the globe, and by the tender age of nineteen many of them were captains. After long, distinguished careers, most of them eventually retired back to Scilly, where I am told the whole row of homes along Church Street was lived in almost exclusively by retired ships' captains. Even now, the relatively new homes at the top of Church Road are called Pilots' Retreat, in recognition of this impressive nautical heritage.

Sailing is still very much in the blood here. Children brought up from a young age to steer on the water do it as second nature. And some things don't change: it is still the case that many young men and women from here join the Navy or Merchant Navy and spend the early years of their adult life sailing around the world. They return to

Scilly on their shore leave and it is good to see them home safely, laden with adventures in distant ports.

Learning to pilot a small boat is not overly hard, but it does take some getting used to. It's a bit like patting your head and rubbing your tummy at the same time. Once you have nailed it, you never lose the skill. It is different from steering a car or bike. These vehicles respond immediately to the turn of the steering wheel. Turn to the left and the front wheels point left. The front drags the rear, which swings round to follow the line the front axle is taking. This is all very responsive and there is no time-lag. The tyres are gripping the road – there is no skid or sideways travel. The road itself is not in motion, unlike the sea, which moves this way and that and up and down, both with currents and with the swell. The wind does not generally have a bearing on a car's direction, but it has a dramatic effect when sailing. The rudder of a boat is at the rear, so it is the stern that swings round and points the bow in the direction of travel. Turning a boat is like steering on grease. There is a time-lag between moving the rudder and the boat changing direction. An added complication with a boat comes when steering from the tiller at the rear, instead of a steering wheel at the front. Push the tiller to starboard and the boat turns to port, and vice versa. It all takes some concentration at first. If you have ever tried riding one of those circus bicycles that have the front steering rigged to turn in the opposite direction from the way the handlebars are twisted, then you will get my meaning. I was looking forward to teaching Lewis and Bella all about this. There is no fun better than messing about in boats.

Like most of the boatmen here, Fraser Hicks could drive

a boat before he could walk. At sea for most of his adult life, he is a man with brackish blood. His father before him, Mike Hicks, was a boatman, too – one of the originators of the St Mary's Boatmen Association, and chairman of the council. Like all boatmen, both men are supremely able at sea. It was when Mike gave Fraser his first driving lesson in a car that their combined abilities behind the wheel came unstuck. Fraser tells of the first driving lesson his father gave him. Approaching the first corner, a left-hand bend, Fraser turned the steering wheel to the left thirty yards before the actual turning – just as he would have done behind the wheel of his boat, *Sea King*. The car did what was asked of it and plunged into the hedge, well before the bend. Nobody was hurt, there were only bruised egos; but not bruised that much. Fraser happily recounts this story to his passengers with a level of self-deprecating humour. Not to passengers in his car, mind you, only ones in his boat, obviously.

Unlike a car, there is no requirement for a boat licence in the UK. Anyone can buy a dinghy and sail it, without even knowing how to tie a basic knot or how to approach a mooring. There are so many things to think about on the water. I have a modicum of boating experience and a power-boat qualification. I'm a broadly competent sailor who sometimes overestimates his capabilities. I had owned a few small motor boats, and on returning to Scilly I made it a priority to get a family boat.

There is no economy in owning a pleasure boat. Never fool yourself that you are saving money by owning one. Absolutely everything about boating is colossally expensive. The engines guzzle fuel; the moorings cost an arm and a leg; a length of rope from the chandler's will set you back the cost of a perfectly healthy kidney, for instance. The boats themselves can be relatively cheap, but they are the loss-leaders. They are like printers for your computer: you buy the latest inkjet printer for a pittance, just to find that once the complimentary ink cartridge has run out, you have to take on night-shifts at the supermarket stacking shelves to earn enough for a refill.

Ah, but you can use a pleasure boat to catch fish – and fish is expensive to buy. The cost of the boat can be recouped in that way. However, the economics of taking up fishing don't stack up. Factor in the price of the lost fishing tackle to the mix, and this will outweigh the cost of the catch, for the day-fisherman. Bang your chest, like the big Neanderthal provider you might think you are, but do not be delusional. It would have been far more economical to travel on a first-class return ticket from Scilly to the nearest Fortnum & Mason to buy a fillet of smoked Scottish salmon and a bottle of Moët. There would have been change, too. Far cheaper, but arguably far less fun.

It is said that the second-best day of your life is when you buy a boat. The best day is when you sell it. There is still no feeling like it, though, and within a few months of arriving back in Scilly I had bought a sixteen-foot motor boat. A Sheltie with a sixty-horsepower Yamaha outboard, just perfect for family trips to other islands and fishing expeditions. I kept her on a mooring in the middle of the harbour. A year later I bought a second boat, a small eleven-foot fibreglass punt that had been owned by a succession of St Mary's boatmen over the years. With a four-horsepower engine, it was perfect for calm days and trips around the harbour – far more manageable for the children to use and learn in. This boat we kept on a running line along the harbour's edge at Town Beach.

I have had my share of mishaps, but fortunately no sinkings. Well, one, but that doesn't really count.

The Police team built a raft for a regatta in the harbour. We scavenged two tin baths and an old windsurfing board. When finished, the raft was big enough to fit five of us on it, and furthermore it floated. For a while. Before a crowd of several hundred jeering onlookers, six teams paddled for victory around the harbour. Some crews were clearly built for speed. Others, like the Fire and Rescue team, simply relied on superior weaponry and fire-power. They had fixed an auxiliary pump to their craft and set about hosing everyone else down. Generally people like to sock it to the police, whenever there is a 'friendly' event, so we bore the brunt of their fire-power. They promptly filled our bathtubs, to much cheering and laughter from the quay, and we sank. I guess that was the object really, and for the life of me to this day I do not know what it was all in aid of. Probably the Lifeboats, because they like to take part in events they can win. They duly won.

Our lifeboat and its voluntary crew do a remarkable job, however. I have seen them put out in some of the most treacherous seas. I have never had to use them, touch wood, but I am glad they are here. I have been lost in the fog once or twice, and it is easy to do. It is best not to do it while your mother-in-law is in the boat with you, though. When I am on-duty I do not use my own boat. I travel on a variety of local boats, just like everyone else. It makes more sense.

I decided on a whim, one early shift, to travel to one of the smaller inhabited islands for a spot of foot patrol. A deep-red sunset over the island of Samson had correctly predicted a horizon-to-horizon duck-egg-blue sky and an oil-slick-smooth sea by sunrise over the Eastern Isles. Once the light sea mist had burnt off, it would deepen the blue and be a surefire brilliant day. The conditions were perfect for being outside. It was too good an opportunity to miss, not to be a police officer on a tropical island that day. I 'eeny, meeny, miny, moed' which island I should go to and settled on St Martin's. If the need to go there were questioned, I could blame my visit on the necessity to lower the teetering pile of routine firearms enquiries that our 'in-tray' had amassed over the weeks. Home visits were needed to check on shotgun certificate-holders' weapon security.

Planning an off-island trip is a dark art. There is a whole bundle of logistical considerations in popping to one of the other islands, which have very little to do with actual policing and everything to do with the weather, the state of the sea and the mode of transport. There is no simply getting into a squad car and driving down the road. That would get me as far as the end of the quay, and no further. Whichever way I look at it, no fewer than two boat trips are necessary. One out and one back. Sometimes more, if visiting a sequence of islands, where there is a need to change at different quays.

The interconnectedness of boats and the associated conditions can be complex – not unlike travelling between lines on the London Underground. On arrival in Scilly, the metropolitan brain initially needs to relearn navigation, not from an iconic schematic Underground map, but by line of sight, dead-reckoning and a common-sense regard for weather and tides. I frequently find myself on the quay in uniform, mingling with the bewildered, newly arrived visitors. They charmingly view me as they would the conductor at Waterloo Station.

'Good morning, Officer. My family and I have just arrived on holiday from South Kensington. Would you be good enough to tell us which boat we get on, to travel to St Martin's?'

'No problem at all, sir. You have just missed the tripper boat *Golden Spray*, which was going there direct. You will now have to travel on several boats. Take the *Spirit* to St Agnes, but don't get off; stay on it while it takes a sightseeing trip around the Western Isles. It will call in at Rushy Bay on Bryher on the way back. Disembark here and wade ashore. Hug the coast for a mile anticlockwise to Anna-Quay. There you catch *Tornado* for the short hop over to New Grimsby on Tresco. Cut across the island on foot to Old Grimsby, to board *Cyclone* to Lower Quay on St Martin's. You should make it by dark. Good luck!'

In non-urgent situations we hop on a regular inter-island ferry with the visitors and locals. Once you get your head round the syncopation of tide state with the time of day and weather conditions, it is possible to predict fairly accurately arrival and departure times, along with the destinations for the numerous boats. Many of the more seasoned holidaymakers know the names of the boats and boatmen off by heart, more comprehensively than many locals, in some instances. Travelling by boat as a police officer with the visitors is one of life's professional pleasures for me. These small ferries are all basically open boats, forty-eight to fifty feet in length, with bench seats that expose between seventy-two and one hundred passengers at a time to the elements. Tickets are bought in the morning, after standing in a long, snaking queue of cagoules, buckets and bamboo shrimp-nets at the kiosk on Old Quay. A return trip to the off-islands, all for under a tenner. The occasional comedic salty slosh of sea water over the gunwales is thrown in for free. By the end of a choppy crossing the immaculately coiffed hair hangs limp, on the ones with wet bottoms who chose their seats without regard for the direction of the wind. Forget 'bed head'; here we have 'boat head'. The vessels are all wonderfully different in design and colour. Some are old and wooden and others of more modern fibreglass construction. Each has its own paint scheme that does not change with the decades. They are all supremely seaworthy and well maintained.

The desiccating effects of a lifetime of salt spray, and exposure to the glare of the harsh ultraviolet light, have given the mask of each skipper a serious, ruddy, leathery look. These are Scillonian men who are not known for hogging the bathroom for their morning moisturising regime. Deep crow's feet on their faces provide reassurance that each boat is safe in the hands of decades' worth of squinted concentration, knowing how to read and respect the waters around Scilly. Either that, or the skippers have dreadful moisturising regimes.

I like to board the tripper boats late, after everyone has already taken their seats. I revel in the little gasp of surprise and the darted nervous glances between passengers, as all heads turn to see the rarity of a uniformed bobby clambering aboard amongst them. I frequently see in their eyes that they are wondering if my motives for boarding their boat might have serious implications for them. I play on this. If there is enough tension and attention, I shout across the heads of the visitors, in mock seriousness to the boatman in charge, 'Just spot-checking for passports and vaccinations.' If I pitch it right, with a straight face, the more gullible tourists take on a look of panic, as they turn to their partner to remonstrate that it was *their* job to find out these details – and now they are going to get arrested.

Of course there are no such requirements on Scilly. It is a benign environment, as much England as the Isle of Wight is, but it does have the feel of being abroad, so I get away with this joke more often than is credible. Once that mirth is out of the way, the tension subsides and my presence on the boat becomes run-of-the-mill. My helmet frequently gets passed around the children during the trip, while I enjoy a relaxed, wide-eyed grilling from adult passengers about my job for the duration of the journey. Mostly these are predictable questions that I never really tire of.

'How many of you are there?' To which I pedantically give the literal answer, 'Just one of me.'

Then we dance around their intended meaning of the word 'you', and I eventually give the answer they actually wanted.

'There's three police officers, a Police Community Support Officer and currently one Special Constable.'

'Why are there policemen on Scilly when there is no crime?' Illogically followed by: 'What if something happens on St Mary's while you are on an off-island for the day?'

I sort my way through all the questions, without maintaining a right to silence or legal representation, until we arrive at our destination and disperse for our various adventures. After a few hours I invariably find myself on the same boat back with the same passengers, so my passport and vaccines joke only works on the outward trip. The wet-bottomed visitors have all dried out by now, but have abandoned any pretence at looking immaculate. They sport salty tide-lines on their clothing, like tie-dye hippies, and have thrown caution to the wind with trousers at half-mast and sand in their turn-ups. When I see this, I know the islands are working their magic on them and that the process of deep relaxation is bedding in. They will sleep better that night than they have done for months.

The return journey to St Mary's sees visitors deep in thought, dreaming of escaping the rat race. They have spent the last four hours thinking 'what if', and calculating the equity from the sale of their homes in the Cotswolds or the South East. The questioning becomes more practical and hints at their daydreams. As a consequence, I step outside my policing role and take on a more consultative role. 'Does the plane fly throughout the year?' 'Where do the children go to school?' and 'How much would a flower farm cost to buy?'

One of the questions I often get asked is whether we have a police boat, and wouldn't it be sensible if we did have one? I'm not convinced it would. Scilly can be a treacherous place for boatmen, and police officers are not trained as boatmen. Many centuries ago the Admiralty charted the coast of England, Wales and Scotland. They graded the coast from one to ten, with ten being reserved for the most dangerous navigable coastline. They started north of Scilly and worked clockwise around Britain, so Scilly was one of the last places they surveyed. When they got round to assessing our waters, the Admiralty realised that the rocks, sandbanks, currents and weather out here were another notch up on the scale of peril. Scilly was graded eleven.

There was a police boat several decades ago, in the era before health-and-safety risk assessments became something that troubled the thought processes of a cunning plan. A blue-and-yellow Battenberg-liveried fourteen-foot skiff, with a nippy twenty-five-horsepower Mariner engine. One day in the late 1980s the local Police Sergeant was asked by the police protection officers of the Protestant evangelist and Ulster Unionist MP, Reverend Dr Ian Paisley, if the MP could be taken to St Martin's for the day. The Ulsterman was holidaying on Scilly, as many VIPs have done (and still do), and his security status demanded that he could not travel on one of the regular tripper boats. This would have been one of those days when an assessment of the tide state should have returned the answer 'No can do', but as can be the way with police, we often don't like to tell it as it is, to VIPs. Too eager to please.

The sea was dropping on an exceptionally low spring tide, and navigating the few miles across the shallow water between St Mary's and St Martin's would have been discounted by experienced boatmen. The sergeant set off from the harbour with Dr Paisley on board, surrounded by his humourless bodyguards, wearing their over-bulky breast-pocketed two-piece suits that summer's day. As the boat passed the Crow Point just off Pendrethan and committed to the leg of the journey that would see it across the sandflats to Higher Town, it ran aground on a sandbank and stuck there fast, unable to go forward or back. The boat was in a foot of water, with the tide receding. They were essentially all safe, as it was calm, but they were going nowhere.

All but the Reverend took off their shoes and socks, rolled up their trousers and stepped out of the boat into the shallow water, half a mile out to sea. Archimedes' principle did its thing, and the hull of the boat lifted a little off the sand, enabling it to be pushed, but the water was still too shallow to consider using the outboard motor. For the next couple of hours the protection officers and the sergeant pushed the boat and its increasingly unimpressed occupant at a slow, tortuous trudge, the mile and a half to St Martin's. I am informed by a source close to the action that the distinctly unimpressed firebrand-preacher provided no-nonsense, career-limiting feedback throughout.

I am sure any connection would have been denied, but the police boat was taken out of service on Scilly shortly afterwards. The practicalities of having our own boat for police work don't stack up, either. If we were to sail to another island to make an arrest, then there would be no ability to safely manage the prisoner on the way back, if we were concentrating on driving. Even the process of mooring up is complex.

On one occasion Mat and I had to get to one of the off-islands in a hurry, without being announced. We needed to locate a suspect for an offence and search their house before the potential for evidence was lost. There was always the risk that if we just hopped on a normal boat, the purpose of our journey would be frustrated. The jungle drums would have beaten and a call might have been made ahead to alert the suspect that we were on our way. There were no tripper boats scheduled to be going to the island, so there was no option other than to consider using my little punt that particular day. I reasoned that it was a very calm day – with oily, flat seas in fact. The weather was predicted to stay fine, which it did, and the tides were just dropping. A lovely day for boating. I was qualified, and both of us were trained in sea survival. This is not training that teaches you how to catch rainwater, or which crewmate to eat first; it is simply about surviving mishaps that mostly involve getting wet and cold. We were travelling in plain clothes, with lifejackets, and to all intents and purposes were just off out on a mackerel-fishing trip together.

There was little preparation that we needed to do. We packed the paperwork we required in Mat's backpack and collected a lifejacket each from my garage. Down on Town Beach, I pulled the boat in on her running line, to find that she was still half-full of fishing tackle from an excursion I had made the day before. Mat and I removed our shoes and socks, rolled up the legs of our jeans and waded into the shallows to hop aboard the little open boat, as she bobbed in the shallows. It was as far as it is possible to get from jumping in a patrol car to set off on an enquiry, as we would have done on the mainland.

With people watching us with curiosity from Holgates Green, overlooking the harbour, I started the engine and we set off confidently, in a tiny boat propelled by a five-horsepower engine. The going was slow and, with the current against us, we were making less than six knots. Although it was calm, Mat, who was seated in the bow, took a wave from the wash of a larger boat that we passed just as we left the harbour. He was soaked from the chest down within five minutes of setting off. We ploughed on regardless.

Our journey took us three-quarters of an hour, which was just enough time for Mat to dry out. When you reach your destination in a car, you just pull up at the side of the road, turn off the engine and get out. With a boat it is not so easy. A top tip is to wait for the skipper to let you know when you can, or cannot, get off. There is always someone who is a bit over-eager to manfully toss some luggage, a dog or a child ashore while the boat is still moving. Mat was that man on this occasion. Seeing the quay approach, he went to hurl the backpack containing our papers ashore. He completely misjudged it, and what should have been an easy three-foot throw turned into a two-foot plop into the water, for our bag of papers. I had not brought the boat to a halt, so we simply carried on and overshot, while the bag absorbed water and started to disappear beneath the surface, like Leonardo DiCaprio in *Titanic*. With my very own Kate Winslet still at the bow, I managed to do a full circle and hold the boat over the spot where we had last seen Leonardo, the bag. For the second time that journey Mat got wet, dunking his arms into the sea to grapple for the bag before it was lost for ever. Unlike in the film, this Winslet did manage to rescue DiCaprio and pulled it back on board to resuscitate it. I went back to the quay, and this time Mat waited until we were firmly tied up before getting himself and the bag ashore.

That left me just sitting in the boat without any way of getting ashore. I was not allowed to tie up along the quay, as it is a working quay and other boats need access to it to pick up and disgorge their cargoes and passengers. No, what I needed to do was motor ashore to the beach, lifting and killing the engine at the last minute so that it did not ground out and bend the propeller. This was an easy option for me. I had done it many hundreds of times, having been taught by Ogilvy Volcere, a Seychellois Creole boatman and good friend on the island of Aride in the Seychelles, which I was warden of in the early 1990s. We had a surf-landing to that beach every time, and the action looks spectacular when done on a beach with powerful waves. The technique is to wait at the back of the surf and observe the pattern of the sets of waves. When you know you can accurately predict the largest wave, you let it pass beneath the boat, then gun the engine to follow it in, between it and the following wave. You ride on its back just as it breaks, kill the engine and tilt the propeller out of the water. This takes some practice and is best done standing. Ogilvy used to do it perfectly every time, with a lit cigarette that he had rolled while watching the waves hanging out of his mouth, like Andy Capp. The momentum of the boat riding on the top of the surf drives the boat up the beach high enough so that the subsequent wave does not follow on and swamp you and, worse still, drag you backwards.

The wave conditions on the beach that day in Scilly were a very pedestrian two to three inches. So my prowess at beach-surf entry was going to be a damp squib. There was no powerful wave to drive me up the beach, so I ground to a halt in a foot of water on the shallow sloping beach. I had to get out and, in bare feet, painfully and awkwardly pick my way across the sharp barnacle-covered pebbles to wade ashore for twenty yards, pulling the boat behind me. Ogilvy would have dropped his head in shame. The boat was heavy, so I could only grind it ashore far enough to push its nose out of the water at the tide-line.

We went off and did our policing business successfully, to return an hour later and find the boat high and dry, with the tide having receded fifty yards. I had committed the first sin of boating: don't ground your boat. It was far too heavy to move. We were stranded on the beach until the tide came back to refloat her a couple of hours later. Several tripper boats came and went in that time. Each and every one of the skippers saw my basic error and tutted, I have no doubt. The period of inactivity in the sun gave Mat a second chance to fully dry out that day.

We got back to St Mary's eventually, having soaked Mat for the third and final time. He had to push the boat out of the shallows so I could lower the engine, getting immersed up to his waist in the process. I always get the feeling that nothing I do in boats is done out of the glare of the professional boatmen here. Had we been scored out of ten for boating competency I think we would have perhaps secured a marginal three. For comedic effect I reckon a creditable nine or ten. It is only the visitors who ask why we don't have our own police boat. The locals already know the answer.

LOVELY DAY FOR BOATING

On my days off during the summer I like to go fishing at sea. I don't really care if I catch or not – that is not the point. The act of getting in a boat and steaming out into the sound off St Mary's is a thrill for me like little else. I have fished ever since I was a child: at first from the quayside for crabs to fill my bucket; and then, a little older, in a boat with Dad and Mum for mackerel in Looe Bay. Bobbing several miles from shore, drifting this way and that, surrounded by islands at every point of the compass, is magic. Nothing puts me at greater ease than this.

I like watching out for the telltale signs of gannets in the distance, hitting on shoals of fish, so that I can get in amongst them and drop a line of feathered hooks. When the gannets do not show, I will head for my favourite spots, such as Spencer's or Spanish Ledge, or out at the Eastern Isles if I have enough time and fuel. There I can be fairly sure of catching pollock or perhaps getting in amongst mackerel. Every so often I may hit codling or red gurnard, which are excellent eating, too. An hour's trip in the boat on a really good day will see me filleting fish for the freezer for two hours. If there are no fish, which is rare, I just watch the seals.

I prefer not to be alone in the boat. Partly for safety, but mostly because an event shared is an adventure. Alone it is just a story. There needs to be a witness to the one that got away, or the pod of dolphins surfacing on the bow, or the six-foot-wide lazy sunfish basking at the surface that didn't notice us until we drew alongside. Watching people catch their first fish ever in their lives is as thrilling to me as catching my own first fish. They always ask me, 'How will I know I have a fish?'

To which my answer is always, 'I will know first, because you will start squealing like a child.' And they do. If the line pulls strongly for several tugs in the hand, then falls heavy and vertical with the occasional tug, you have a sluggish pollock. If the line dances with greater excitement, and stays rapidly tugging as you reel in, sometimes pulling the line all round the side of the boat, you have mackerel. In the summer when the sea heats up, the mackerel can be caught just below the boat, in full view. They splash deep crimson blood on the deck and on our clothes as they are hauled aboard, before they are quickly dispatched with a crack of the neck. It sounds gruesome, but it is the raw end of eating: from free swimming to fresh food in under a minute. Although many people are squeamish at first, I have never had anyone turn down fresh fried mackerel and buttered bread, just an hour out of the sea.

Fish are readily abundant in the summer. With three people fishing, the gannets locating the fish, and me dispatching the catch, we can bring aboard forty fish in twenty minutes. Then everyone gets fresh fish for dinner, including the neighbours around the police station along Jerusalem Terrace and the gulls at sea, which guzzle down the heads, tails and guts as I steam home, topping and tailing on the way. When the water is cooler, earlier in the season, the line has to be dropped to a count of fourteen 'Mississippis' before there is the chance of a catch. The pollock are just off the bottom, where the whales are. If it feels as if you have caught a whale, you have in fact snagged the bottom and will most probably lose a lead (£1), a swivel (30p) and a set of feathers (£1). At Bishop Rock, eight miles from St Mary's, I lost the whole lot when I snagged a reef: line (£5), rod (£40) and reel (£60). It all just slipped out of my hands, which were slippery with the slime from a previously caught pollock, and sank into the depths amongst the wrecks of Sir Cloudesley Shovell's doomed fleet.

Being out in a boat is also where I am almost assured of not having to be a police officer. Nobody ever sidles up and has a hypothetical conversation about some aspect of my work. On the few occasions two boats occupy the same patch of sea, each observes a voluntary exclusion zone around the other's boat that is respected. When two people chat face-to-face in a pub, it feels a bit of an invasion of one's personal space if one person gets closer than about eighteen inches. With boats that is extended to about fifty yards. This makes a casual whispered conversation to me, about the neighbour's poor parking or intemperate nocturnal habits, quite impossible. I say I am 'almost' assured of not being bothered, but I do still carry my mobile phone, so that Comms can contact me. I hardly ever get calls normally, so when it rings it is almost certainly Plymouth Control Room or one of my colleagues on Scilly requiring my assistance. Even when out on the boat, I am back-up to the on-duty officer, my neighbour, my colleague, my friend. If they need help, regardless of what I am up to, I drop everything and go. This is just part of the post out here. I accept it gladly, although interrupting boating time is perhaps the most inconvenient.

I have been called back to dry land in a hurry to back up colleagues in all sorts of incidents, from assaults to shoplifting, each time turning up fresh from the boat, still smelling slightly of fish, with sand in my hair and mackerel blood-splashes on my face and hands. My slightly crazed, salty, dishevelled, bloodied appearance seems to have a calming affect on the suspect.

On Father's Day in May 2014 the family took me out on our boat for a special treat. Sarah had been to the Farm Deli and Tanglewood Kitchen in town and had purchased some treats to make me a special picnic aboard. We anchored up in calm waters to the south of Tresco on a beautiful day. The water was clearer than I have ever seen it. Crystal-clarity to the seabed twenty feet below the boat, and still as a mill-pond. We could watch fish swimming underneath as we tucked into our cheeses, pickles, cured meats and olives. It was one of those Sundays when everyone was out in their boats doing the same. All maintaining their discreet exclusion zones. We stayed basking in the sun or dipping our toes off the edge of the boat into the water for hours at anchor. It was perfect. The best Father's Day present ever, without question. To make it just that little bit extra-special I suggested that we finish up with a short spot of fishing, to see if we could catch dinner. It was my day, so everyone agreed. Once the anchor was aboard, I motored a couple of miles to the

Bartholomew Buoy, a spot directly between St Mary's and St Agnes. The tide was running perfectly for there to be a chance of a shoal of mackerel at this spot. I turned off the engine to drift with the strong tide and got the lines ready. Just before dropping the first set of hooks, my mobile rang.

It was not Comms, as I had anticipated with little relish. It was my mum in Devon. She broke the news that she had been with Dad. He had just passed away that morning in the nursing home – the merciful end to his long suffering with dementia.

There is no perfect time or place for a message like that. Scilly became in an instant even more remote. A call from Comms would have been far more preferable. There was no leaving Scilly on a Sunday to be with Mum. The *Scillonian* did not sail and the planes did not fly. We don't even get Sunday papers until Monday out here. I knew I would not be able to be with her until the next day at the earliest.

The news saw the end to our family day at sea. We headed for harbour. My heart was not in it to stay any longer, although in hindsight I can think of no better place for me to have been, on hearing of Dad's passing. Being on islands and fishing are even more special to me now. I am with him, the former Merchant Navy man, whenever I am at sea.

DRUNKEN MARINERS

Bishop Rock, the westernmost point of the archipelago, is the start or finish for record-breaking transatlantic crossings. When you have reached Scilly, you have reached your final destination; or conversely the place you will be starting from. That must feel odd for people who have still either got a long way to go, before they can lay their head on their own pillow, or who have already travelled several days to get here. This is the shortest point between North America and the UK. Swim due west from here some 2,085 miles and you will haul your freezing goose-fatted carcass up the beach at the small town of Torbay in Newfoundland. If you time your arrival there between 4 and 8 p.m. you will be able to warm up with a stiff Happy Hour drink at Mrs Liddy's, the oldest pub in that part of Canada. Perhaps I can offer this top tip: do not mention you just came from Scilly. The people of Newfoundland lost a large expensive mooring buoy some years back in a storm. It spent a year floating across the Atlantic in the currents to our neck of the woods. The 'finders keepers' rule was invoked by our harbour master and the buoy was recycled and put to use for several years warding boats off Bacon Ledge, a quarter-mile outside St Mary's harbour. It has since been replaced by a different marker and has been retired to dry land. The buoy now serves as a big red seat on Old Quay.

Bishop Rock also lays claim to being the smallest island in the world with a building on it. The building in question is a lighthouse. The rock itself is not so much an island as a wave-pounded lump of granite that pokes up a few feet above high tide. It receives the full fetch of the Atlantic. Even on a calm day the waves surge around it powerfully, making landing on it nigh-on impossible. How they ever built a lighthouse on it, I will never know, but if it were to be done today it would be a considerable undertaking. No seabirds can even nest there because the waves break over the rock. The sides are steep, plunging vertically to the bottom of the black-green sea 130 feet below.

It is worth a trip out to Bishop Rock, if any of the boatmen have chalked up Western Isles trips on the blackboards in Hugh Town. Local folklore has it that the rock was once central to the Scillonian criminal justice process. As a suspect, you would be taken out to the rock in a rowing boat by a lynch mob and left there, with only the barnacles and limpets to take your lead from. Several tides later, the mob would return to see if you had managed to cling on. If you were still there, you would be taken back to dry land. In the grip of that logic, no doubt your survival would be conclusive proof that you were in league with Poseidon, and therefore as guilty as charged. There are no recordings of the outcome in those circumstances, but I very much doubt it included community service or a conditional discharge. If you were missing instead – swept off the rock to a watery grave – then your headstone would probably record that you were an innocent, virtuous soul reclaimed by the mermaids. Either way, those subject to this out-of-court settlement were on a hiding to nothing. The sorts of communities that operated these methods of retribution were looking out for themselves, where they could see no other option. We don't do that any more here, although I have my suspicions that it continues to feature as a potentially viable option for a few folk on some islands.

The lighthouse that stands on the rock is there for a very good reason. It warns ships not only of the rock it stands on, but also of the hundreds of savage rocks to the east of it for several miles. The sea around our coast is treacherous, with protrusions of granite which sometimes lurk just beneath the waves or stand proud of the surface, looking vicious like the grim black teeth in a mythical leviathan. The Western and Norrad (Northern) Rocks have laid claim to many hundreds of ships over the millennia, as have all the lumps and bumps around our coast – ships that had been coming from (or going to) the likes of Bristol or Liverpool, the Americas, Africa and the Mediterranean. Trading, passenger and war ships have all foundered on these rocks and spilt their cargoes to the depths.

Before the era of radio communication, ships foundered in the dark and took their crews with them. Many sailed in calm or storm into our troubled waters and never re-appeared out the other side. Wreckage and bodies, washed up over the following days and weeks, may have hinted at the unseen tragedy, but not necessarily at the whereabouts. There were no black boxes to search for, to locate the site of a sunken ship. There are undoubtedly many ships on the seabed that remain undiscovered. Their perishable cargoes have long since dispersed, but the precious ones of gold and cannons still tempt divers into the depths. Only a couple of years ago a Greek urn was recovered by a local diver in the Tresco Channel. Other finds suggest this was part of the cargo from a ship sailing from the Mediterranean many hundreds of years ago.

Historically islanders scavenged for what the sea gave up, and saved the crews when they could. These are not the Dorset shores of Moonfleet, where crews were tricked with torches from the cliffs. People here did make a concerted effort to save life and limb. To be fair, that may have had a lot to do with the wrecking fees. The smart cookies here realised that they were paid to save cargoes and people. Former generations of Scillonians were adept at filling in the forms to claim wrecker rights – as indeed they still are today. It was then (and occasionally is now) something of an industry here. Land was in short supply to bury bodies, and the extra injection of new genetic stock every now and then was most welcome, no doubt. The Turks Head on St Agnes is not so named for no reason; it is something to do with part of the Spanish Armada wrecking on the shores there in the sixteenth century, and some Moorish crews staying on for the season. For the most part, ships simply never arrived at their destination and nothing more was ever known of them. They were lost at sea somewhere along their route. It is entirely probable that many wrecks still lie undiscovered in the waters around Scilly.

Scilly has seen some record-breaking attempts in the recent past. Always keen to be the first, Richard Branson and his Virgin Atlantic *Challenger* crews have both cried and celebrated here. Initially tears, with *Challenger 1*, which sank 140 miles before Bishop Rock in 1985; and then cheers a year later, with *Challenger II*, which broke the speed record for the 3,500-mile crossing from New York in 1986, in three days and ten hours. Their jubilation on succeeding second time around was short-lived, however, as they were denied the Hales Trophy, an award for the fastest transatlantic crossing in a boat with a commercial maritime purpose. Self-indulgence was evidently not considered to be a commercial maritime purpose, so having not read the small print, their efforts were rejected. To add insult to injury, the *Challenger II* no doubt had to take on more fuel, at St Mary's prices, so that they could push on to the mainland. Here on Scilly, fuel is eye-wateringly expensive. Shipping it to the islands puts a premium on it that rivals the cost of Persian saffron, by weight. The first 3,500 miles of the Virgin trip had been done on subsidised US-priced gas. Receiving the bill for filling the tank here can have only brought a tear to the duct of even the most philanthropic of billionaires.

With the cost of fuel so high, the next record-breaking attempts looked to capitalise on our ample source of wind. We are not in the lee of anything here, so it is a rare day when we are completely becalmed. The south-westerly gales blow strong off the Atlantic, especially in winter. For the remainder of the year it is prone to be breezy here, too, which is an advantage if you own a boat propelled by your own bedding.

The sailor and adventurer Pete Goss, MBE, tried to carve his name in the history books with one fewer boat than Mr Branson. He raised £4 million and had an innovative catamaran built for him in Totnes, to sail in a race around the world faster than anyone had ever done before. It was a simply massive, sleek blue sailboat with long carbon-fibre, wave-piercing hulls and two skyscraper-tall masts set side-by-side. The biggest ocean-racing yacht ever built: an amazingly impressive and beautiful craft that drew huge attention. HM Queen Elizabeth II even got in on the act and launched her. In my view, they gave it a rubbish name – *Team Philips* – but I guess when someone else is paying the bill, they can call it what they want.

In March 2000, Goss brought the yacht to Scilly to take her out for some sea trials, before giving her the off. The catamaran broke. The wave-piercing hulls got pierced by the waves. Goss and his team limped back to port, having snapped the structure like a breadstick. I was off-duty that day and sat watching him from the warm comfort of The Mermaid, pint in hand with the other customers. We saw the sad sight of his shattered dream being towed back to the safety of the harbour by the St Mary's lifeboat.

Ironically the team strapline on the side of Pete's boat was 'Let's Make Things Better'. They should have reread their mission statement when they took the boat back to mend her, for this is evidently what they completely failed to do. Another £250,000 later, and in December of the same year they managed to get 500 miles off Ireland before the catamaran broke again. The crew escaped unharmed on a slow boat to Nova Scotia, and *Team Philips* vanished into the depths. I'm thinking they got lucky, really. If they had set off on the World Race from Barcelona later that month, as envisaged, they would presumably have had to weather Cape Horn and the Roaring Forties in the Southern

Ocean. I wouldn't have given them good odds for that, if they couldn't handle our waters.

'Let's make things better' was also the reassuring sentiment my doctor expressed that same month, when I presented to him, having also been broken by the wind. He diagnosed that I was wearing the wrong hat. The inside of my ears had become irritated from being outside, on foot patrol, exposed to the elements for too long. The constant tempest rushing past my lugholes, trying to get a tune out of me (like a milk bottle) for weeks, had seriously irritated the nerve endings in my inner ear, hypersensitising them. This in turn had caused my scalp to become hypersensitive, as if I was constantly having an Indian head-massage with Deep Heat. The GP prescribed that on blustery days I ditch the tall helmet, which simply perches on the top of my head. Instead, he instructed, I should wear a woolly hat, pulled down firmly over my ears. The pharmacy couldn't do me a bobble hat on prescription, so I ordered a black knitted one with the word POLICE on it, from Headquarters clothing stores. I patrolled in it for the rest of the winter.

Both Mr Branson and Mr Goss can rest easy, however. They merely follow in an esteemed line of maritime mishaps in these waters, occurring over the centuries. Their efforts at world record-breaking ocean-based follies pale into insignificance when compared with that of Sir Cloudesley Shovell. While the modern adventurers lost one boat apiece, the fateful Mr Shovell lost four in one night. What is known is that this experienced Admiral of the Fleet wrecked his boat, HMS *Association*. It hit the Western Rocks, as did the rest of his warships, HMS *Romney*,

Firebrand and *Eagle*. All four ships sank, with the loss of between 1,400 and 2,000 souls, on 22nd October 1707. This is recorded as one of the worst maritime disasters in the history of the British Isles. Sir Cloudesley met his death that night. What did it for him was not an oversight of the small print, or a touching faith in composite design technology, but a basic lack of ability to calculate longitude accurately. He had not known he was off-course.

After the tragedy, the Admiralty put up a reward for the inventor who could come up with a way of calculating longitude, but it was another thirty years before John Harrison came up with a solution: the marine chronometer, a sophisticated clock that was accurate on long sea journeys. Cloudesley Shovell didn't go down with his ship. Legend here has it that he made it ashore to the lawless lands of Scilly, only to be murdered at the top of the beach by a local peasant woman who wanted to steal his priceless emerald ring. A headstone still stands at Porthellic beach, marking the spot where he was buried. He's not there now. Some Londoners came and carted him off to Westminster Abbey, for a proper burial for a man who sank a fleet.

More recently the MV *Cita*, a 3,000-tonne cargo ship, wrecked up onshore on St Mary's in March 1997, sinking and losing its cargo, with thankfully no loss of life. Wikipedia records the charitable efforts of locals who 'assisted in the clean-up operation'. It is on record that no prosecutions were brought under the Merchant Act of 1894 for looting, so clearly everything was above board, and I applaud that. I mention this because, interestingly, the date of this event coincided with an unusual phenomenon, in which almost all the vehicles on the islands got new tyres.

The wreck therefore foretold of improvements in road safety. Coincidentally and irrelevantly, I am informed that this date also saw the almost universal replacement of interior doors and computer mice, with everyone wearing the same plimsolls and T-shirts. Uncannily, a similar cargo to that of the MV *Cita*.

Following the *Cita* onto the rocks was a fog-bank. Timed to perfection, it effectively sealed off Scilly for days, while the locals made like leafcutter ants and carted off the cargo away from the shore, to a hundred hidden garages around the islands. The conditions meant that the police were unable to fly in further officers to help manage the security of the jettisoned cargo. The tide and currents moved the flotsam and jetsam across a wide area. A few extra officers made it across on the ferry, but the police cordon was stretched to frankly meaningless levels.

In these circumstances the job of the police is to act for the Receiver of Wrecks. We look to ensure that those claiming salvage do so lawfully. This was a new one for the police here at the time. There had been no recent precedence for the actions we needed to take. The legal department at Headquarters in Exeter thumbed through the law books and concluded that our best option was to hand out fliers to the pillagers, with details of their obligations under the law and how to notify the Receiver of Wrecks about what they had salvaged. The Receiver then makes contact with the owner of the goods, and a financial settlement is arranged for the scavengers. The photocopier was set to work and a batch of fliers was produced and speedily sent to the scene, where they were handed to the pillagers as they arrived.

Physically, the few officers here could not hold back the hordes, who could in effect remove whatever they wished, on the understanding that they reported their findings in full. Satisfied that they were fulfilling their duty as best they could, the officers who were standing point made themselves useful as guides. 'Are you here for the wreck, sir? Here is a notice to tell you what you must do, if you recover anything. You will find interior mahogany doors over there to the left, plimsolls and car tyres to the right. I'm afraid all the golf bags have been snapped up, but could we interest you in a box of computer mice? I think there are some left.'

It was a very effective clean-up, all things considered. It was as if a spoonful of sugar had been scattered on an ants' nest – all gone within the blink of an eye. Many items of clothing were washed ashore from containers that had fallen from the deck and split open. The currents carried the T-shirts to all the beaches around the coast. The local women mobilised and the shirts were collected up, washed and dried, then dispatched en masse to orphanages in Romania. A very touching and altruistic act, which gives new meaning to laundering ill-gotten gains.

1997 was quite a long time ago now, and whereas I am certainly not wishing for another wreck, some tyres on some vehicles are looking worn and could do with replacing. The *Cita* now lies at rest about sixty yards off the coast, and I am advised that all its cargo has been removed. New tyres are best ordered through the established routes.

For such a bustling place, it is perhaps surprising that there is no permanent Customs post here, having been disbanded in the early part of this century. The Customs House still stands, alongside Town Beach at Holgates Green, although it is now a set of plush self-catering apartments. The Scillonians have finally seen off the Customs man from their shores. The UK Border Agency (as Customs is currently known) now patrols in fast ships around the coast of the UK. There are five of these cutters in the Visa and Immigration fleet, which pitch up here sporadically throughout the year. The officers either arrive in their ships or by plane, to check out foreign-registered cruise ships or other vessels making to our shores from foreign climes. They generally pop into the police station for a cuppa and a catch-up, or to ask for a few extra hands with their latest task. This has seen us boarding cruise ships from France or Canada and assisting Immigration in setting up a passport control.

On these mutual-aid trips we get ferried out to the larger ship, moored several miles offshore in deeper waters, in the early morning. There we board and set up a passport control, checking the passenger manifold against the passengers on board, who parade before us. The Canadian boats provide the best coffee, and the liners from France the best croissant breakfast. After these administrative duties we check the quarters of the crew. These fall into two brackets. The officer class, who sail and administer the ship, will generally be from the country of origin: French for a French cruiser, and Canadian or American for ships from their respective ports. They have their own berths relatively high up the ship, perhaps with a porthole. The lower-ranking crew are more often than not Filipino, with their quarters in the bottom, near the bilges of the ship. With several people to a room, they inhabit a cramped world, with claustrophobic shoulder-width aisles running the length of their deck. This seems to mimic my stereo-typical view of how I perceive their lives to be, back in the hustle and bustle of the markets of Manila.

The Filipinos have developed a fascinating culture on board. I have observed, on more than one occasion, that generally the carpenter's workshop doubles up as both a place of industry and the main social gathering place for the hundreds of Filipino crew. Crammed in amongst benches, with lathes, vices, band-saws, chisels, hammers, tins of glue, paint, screws and nails, are greasy shelves packed tightly with thousands of recorded copies of old horse races and karaoke DVDs. The carpenter has constructed one thin cabinet to have a Perspex window to keep the dust off the forty-eight-inch flatscreen TV with DVD player. On the floor, with their legs in an inch of wood shavings, are stools and other crude seating for the revellers. It is not a place of safety, with so many sharp tools to hand, but it is a place where it is evident the crews cram themselves in, after the day's shift has been completed, for an evening of raucous entertainment. Long into the night they party, betting on races where the outcome is known to those long-in-the-tooth, then singing their hearts out into the small hours. This is a dry place. No alcohol is drunk or cigarettes smoked, for fear of disorder or fire. We check a sample of DVDs for unlawful material, and some of the cabins for more than their allowance of cigarettes. It is a fascinating insight into a colourful floating culture, which the brilliant-white exterior of the ships give no hint of and the passengers aboard do not see. I enjoy working with the Customs teams and grab the chance, whenever asked, to help them out.

This has even included seizing a yacht. A stricken lone mariner had been towed back to safe harbour. He had radioed Falmouth Coastguard for assistance when he was within range of the RNLI Severn-class lifeboat here on St Mary's. The *Whiteheads* lifeboat put to sea and towed him back to safe harbour, where we could see the effects that a bad storm had had on his boat. His mast was fully ripped off, so he had effected a crude jury-rig: a temporary short mast with just enough height to attach a bit of a sail, to keep the vessel making slow headway in the direction of the prevailing wind. Think of the sail that Tom Hanks managed to cobble together on the raft he made in *Castaway* and you would not be a million miles away.

His arrival occurred a day before the Customs clipper was due to come to Scilly. Part of Customs' duties include boarding yachts that have come from foreign ports to check their crew and documents, and the check for contraband. They got wind of the stricken yachtsman and contacted me to ask that I seize his yacht. They dragged up a piece of legislation I had never used before, which meant they could authorise me to be a Customs officer for the day, or something like that. I was also asked to make a cursory search of the vessel, just in case there were obvious irregularities on board, which might otherwise be hidden before the revenue man could get there and make a thorough search. The Customs' plan was to steam full ahead for the islands and take over from me the next day.

I was more than happy to oblige. This was all new to me: seizing boats and going aboard to search. I went down to the harbour, to find the craft moored up alongside the quay. It was easy to identify amongst the other boats: it was the one that looked as if it had been adrift for several weeks, after getting caught up in a gale; a large white nondescript catamaran with its main mast looking sad and broken, tangled up in rigging and lashed to the side of the boat. The sailor was sitting on the deck, laying out his sodden, crumpled clothing to dry in the sun. He looked dishevelled, trying to tidy up the deck of his battered catamaran.

I shouted down to him, 'Ahoy! Can I come aboard?' It was satisfyingly appropriate terminology in the circumstances, and I wanted to give the impression of not being a novice to this lark.

The young dishevelled Englishman welcomed me onto his deck. He seemed a little nervous. Was he just a beaten man after his ordeal, or was something else afoot? I wondered. He offered me a mug of tea, which I accepted; and then I seized his boat, which he accepted. Both he and it were a right old mess. He had been snatching brief catnaps when the weather conditions permitted, and dozing in soaked bedding for weeks. The storm that he had been caught up in had tumbled his catamaran around. Every item not bolted down was strewn across his living quarters.

I started a search, as I had been asked to do. He watched me. There was nothing obviously out of place, to start with. His papers seemed to be in order, and his story had the ring of truth about it. He had been in the Caribbean, then sailed across to the Azores. From there he set out for the UK, but got caught in a storm, was battered about a bit and drifted for several weeks. I moved on to search his galley. The kitchen drawers and cupboards revealed nothing. It was self-evident that he was pretty short of food, so it was his good luck that he was now safely on dry land. I moved to the fridge and opened the door. There was hardly any food in there, save for a half-open jar of mouldy pâté and something that may have been of green vegetable origin, putrefying in a pool of ooze in the bottom salad compartment. This sailor was not on a gourmet cruise. Other than that, there was nothing in the fridge, apart from what was obviously a large, crudely wrapped cellophane package of cocaine.

I closed the fridge door and moved on to search his bunk. No, really. I'm a policeman, for pity's sake: was I really going to ignore that? With gloved hands, I reached into the fridge and pulled out the big, baby-marrow-shaped wrap of compressed white matter. I found myself holding what I could only suppose was at least two kilos of the purest South American cocaine. At current street prices, it must have been worth £100,000.

I confess I did feel a tingle of excitement. I'll go further than that: I did a little dance. Not the sort of dance anyone other than another police officer would notice. To normal human onlookers, I remained resolutely steely-faced and unruffled. To a colleague, the barely perceptible quickening of breath and widening of the pupils would have given away that, in my mind, I was really doing a conga around the deck. All officers do this little invisible dance when they make a find during a search. I had just hit upon a meaty seizure of drugs.

I looked over at the sailor, half-expecting him to be ready for fight or flight, or training an Uzi on me. He looked back at me and shrugged resignedly. He knew what I was thinking.

'It's not what you think.'

'Go on, educate me.'

'It's a mozzarella.'

It didn't compute at first that he was talking about an actual mozzarella. Why would a dishevelled, shipwrecked, half-starved mariner with a wild-man beard and no appreciable food on board have an unfeasibly large, untouched package of pizza-cheese in his fridge? No, I was on to a drug dealer who was chancing his arm to import coke into the UK – that was obvious. It was clearly the case that 'a mozzarella' was Colombian drug-cartel slang for a two-kilo wrap of coke. Slang that I was previously unaware of. The sort of cover language that Pablo Escobar would have used, to avoid the attentions of the DEA: 'Gringo, ze delivery of fifty mozzarellas will be over the border, *mañana*.'

I think the weary sailor could see my rising scepticism. He explained to me that it was genuinely a catering pack of mozzarella cheese. He recounted how some 600 miles out from land, a container ship had spotted him adrift and drawn alongside. The captain had offered him passage, but he had refused as he didn't want to abandon his ship. They had replenished his stocks of water and given him some food, then waved him on his way. This was the large catering pack of cheese that the ship's chef had tossed down to him before they left him mid-Atlantic. He disliked cheese and had not yet become so famished that he had to resort to eating it. He would have eaten one of his own limbs first. Tentatively I unwrapped a corner and prodded it. It was not powdery, and did indeed have that rubbery bounce of mozzarella. Taking my drug-testing tips more from *Miami Vice* and less from official training manuals, I took a sniff of the contents. I didn't go the whole hog and rub a sample of cheese into my gums, as Crockett or Tubbs would have done, as the smell of poorly refrigerated, three-week-old decomposing curd repulsed me. It gave its game away as to exactly what it was. A little deflated, I stopped dancing.

There were no more surprises on board that I could find, and gradually as I got to know the sailor I realised that his nervous disposition had been because he had hardly slept a wink in four weeks. He seemed like a thoroughly decent chap, who had just had a run of bad luck. And now he had had me clambering all over his world and was facing the prospect of Customs descending on him the next day, and doing the same. As we chatted, he relaxed. I was one of the first people he had had chance to talk to for weeks. I phoned back the master of the Customs clipper to tell him the boat was secure and waiting for them. I gave them a completely truthful update that my cursory search had revealed nothing of merit.

My new friend seemed like a man with a sense of humour. He agreed that as he had no intention of eating the cheese, it was OK that I secrete it in a slightly more incongruous location than the fridge. He showed me a less-obvious hideaway for a block of cheese in the hold, and I tucked it away there. I suspected the next search would be far more thorough than mine. A treat for the Customs officers to find the next day, so that they would have a chance to do their little dance for a moment. I believe Her Majesty's Revenue & Customs favour the cha-cha-cha over the conga.

Pete Goss, the Greek captain of the *Cita* and the skinny mariner are not the only sailors to recognise Scilly as a great place to come ashore. It is a haven for the yachting types. The ones who actually like to sail their boats, that is. As soon as the worst of the winter winds are over, the sailing boats start appearing on our horizon. They arrive from all points of the compass, from many different countries: from the north, for the Irish; the south, for the French; the east, for the Brits; and very occasionally the west, for the drug dealers. Leaving aside the last category, in the main they are a jolly bunch, who are very welcome over here. The flags on their rigging signify the boats' ports of origin, from all over the world.

They moor anywhere they can get anchorage out of the wind. Favoured spots include the Tresco Channel; between the islands of Tean and St Martin's; the sheltered bays at St Agnes, Watermill and Porthcressa; and, most popular, the main Duchy harbour at St Mary's. In the summer there are sometimes several hundred sailing boats anchored around the islands at any one time. Some like to anchor up alone at secluded spots, presumably driven by their own sense of freedom, while others huddle together on the established moorings, to form a like-minded, slightly addled, floating community. All bonded together by the love of being rocked to sleep at night in cramped berths, listening to the clanks of their lanyards slapping against masts. They mostly stay for a few days, then head back home or onwards to another port when the weather is fine, always arriving to coincide with the late afternoon, just in time for a swift gin and tonic. In essence, the boats are expensive excuses for being able to open the cocktail cabinet before 4.30 p.m.

There is a point in the late afternoon, just after the sun

has passed the yardarm, when the waft of zest from sliced limes and the din of ice cubes clinking against crystal glass, coming from the direction of where the boats are anchored, sets off a biological trigger. Like a Pavlovian response, the crews stop what they are doing aboard and get into their little rubber tenders, to come ashore to eat and drink in the bars and restaurants of the island next to which they are moored. On land, they are a distinct group who stick out in appearance from other land-based visitors. Patrolling here gives me an opportunity to observe their appearance and patterns of behaviour. I have noticed that they observe strict national costumes and customs.

British sailors are invariably made up of newly retired couples, or pairs of couples, on a jaunt out to Scilly from Falmouth or Dartmouth. They are in for the early sitting at the restaurants. Many years in the boardroom as CEOs has taught them how to do 'smart casual' with aplomb. The sweater is worn confidently over the shoulders, for both male and female. His shirt is generally vertically striped in pale blue, the shorts salmon-pink, with tanned bare legs that for a whole career were hidden from view beneath a suit and a desk. They protrude unconfidently from the bottom of the turn-ups, extending down to the unsocked, expensive deck-shoes. The women always have perfect hair, gold or pearl bling and mostly white slacks – the least practical colour for boating, which says, 'Look, we can even wear white – we are not grease-monkeys.' There is a new-money brashness about them; it is not disagreeable in the slightest, but very distinct from the other sailors.

I cannot recall ever seeing a French yachtsman not wearing rubber boots. Not just any rubber boots, but narrow, fitted colourful rubber boots with flat soles, gathered at the top around the calf with a drawstring. In every colour but black. It is as if they are worn as a gentle taunt to us Brits: 'You may have taken Napoleon, but we will not wear your wellingtons.' An antidote, perhaps, to our two-fingered salute from Agincourt. They all carry tough waterproof backpacks and wear colourful sou'westers. Travelling in groups of four or five, the French all look tanned, unshaved and lithe; and being all-male crews, they have clearly made the macho decision to dispense with the niceties of regular ablutions. They come ashore to get water, showers and to raid the chandler's for fixings for their boats. They are not fair-weather sailors and put out to sea expertly in stiff winds and choppy seas. They push their boats the hardest, hence the need to fix them when they reach safe harbour. Several times I have been approached on-duty and asked by a Frenchman for an inspirational idea with which to mend their boat, as the bits for the mend at the chandler's are too expensive. There is more than one yacht sailing round the Bay of Biscay with a makeshift transom from an offcut of marine ply from my garage, or an inner-tube bilge-pump seal from my daughter's unused push-bike.

The Irish are my favourite sailors. They are almost always men on a bromance break, away from the confines of domesticity. They are always buoyant and sociable and the first to strike up conversation. They have arrived from Dublin, Wexford or Cork. They are less defined by their clothing, which mostly consists of what they woke up in, as their staying power at the bar. To my mind, they all have the appearance of Christy Moore, and for the remainder of my shift, after meeting and chatting with a group of Irish sailors, I am left humming 'Lisdoonvarna'. Some nights I wish I had been able to book off-duty early and just muscle in with a group of them for the craic, until I have to give up, admit defeat and go home to bed. Sadly, this is not to be, as my role is to be outside the pub and see that nothing happens that might prevent everyone getting safely home.

The Irish are generally the last to leave the pubs for their tiny inflatable dinghies at night, from the pontoon on the quay. As with all nationalities, I like to skulk in the shadows by the railings, casting a concerned eye over them as they make their way home at the end of the night. Watching them tumble, with good humour and much cursing, four at a time into a dinghy made for three. I have observed that there is a direct correlation between the number of pints of Betty Stogs ale they have drunk and the number of times it takes to pull the starter motor to get their outboard working. I have seen them try to start with the motor in gear, which just sends them pitching over each other towards the stern, as the rotor bites the water briefly and lurches the inflatable forward. My favourite is enjoying with them the short-lived moment of triumph as they embark perfectly and take their seats, then start the outboard without a hitch and slip it carefully into gear, before coming to a shuddering halt after two yards, having forgotten to untie the bow line from its mooring ring attached to the pontoon. More than once I have seen a sailor fall into the water, and I am ready to intervene if they are not assisted swiftly to safety by their fellow crewmates. Once they have the tiny outboard going, I keep an eye on them until I lose sight of them, puttering off into the inky black of the unlit harbour to find their boat.

Sailors may place a hefty emphasis on taking on board alcohol in the evening, but there is no lingering in bed in the morning, feeling sorry for themselves. All the yachties are the first to put on hold their self-pitying hangovers and capitalise on the early-morning winds. While most of us are still waiting to stir, as dawn breaks, whichever one of them was appointed Watch the night before is weighing anchor and setting off to the next plotted destination. Their concern is to grab the wind before it calms, as the day warms up and the air becomes still. They may have a long sail ahead of them, or perhaps only a short hop across to another of the archipelago's islands, but whichever is the case, they have to be there before 'gin o'clock'.

STAG ACT

We get our fair share of stag parties here. It is not quite Dublin or Newquay, but nevertheless it does seem to be the case that every so often a group of men descend on us and maraud through town, trying to drink the bars dry. They all fail, for if there is one thing Scilly hardly ever runs short of, it's ale. I use the term 'hardly ever' advisedly, because a number of years ago, after a continued period of bad weather, the supply ship was unable to visit for several weeks. First thing to vanish from the shops was bread, then milk, then fresh veg, followed closely by meat and eggs. Over a period of a week or so the shelves gradually became bare.

There was no particular anxiety about this, except perhaps from the least-productive member of each family – the one who, if the lack of food persisted, would be looked upon as a source of protein. The onset of panic came as the pumps in the pubs started to run dry. Increasingly, beer towels were draped over the handles, as Doom Bar, Betty Stogs, Tribute, HSD, Carlsberg and Carling ran dry. This is the point when the natives became restless and agitated. They were being forced to drink alternative beverages, like wine or cocktails. There was memorable unrest – not quite gatherings of pitchforked protesters, you understand. There could be no focus for the disquiet, after all. It was the weather's fault. Holding Mother Nature to account was going to be a tough call for an angry mob, so the protest didn't develop, but it got close for a while.

Regrettably, stag parties never seem to hit Scilly when the barrels are empty. They are an awkward bunch of people in the main, because their only purpose here seems to be to get drunk. Their planning for the event seems woefully inadequate. As a priority, they consider first their dress code: more than is original, stags opt for a Hawaiian theme. Then comes the mode of transport: almost invariably, they travel on a day-trip here on the ferry from Penzance. On the journey, peer pressure ensures that they avail themselves of the licensed café aboard, so that by the time they disembark they are half-cut. It is at this point that we generally become professionally aware of their presence on the islands, with a few 'Code Blue: there's a stag-do on St Mary's!' phone calls to the station.

Next comes their lunch. This is taken in liquid form, inevitably to levels well beyond their manageable norm. Up to this point it is really much like any standard stag-do: bellow a lot at each other and get drunk. The thing they generally fail to plan adequately for, or fail to grasp, is that if they miss that ferry back to Penzance at 4.30 p.m. they will be stranded on Scilly, in whatever silly costumes they have on, with no accommodation. This then becomes a nightmare for us in the police. We will be the last ones awake and sober to make decisions about their destinies, after they roll out of the pub at midnight and wonder where the burger van is.

There are in fact no fast-food outlets on Scilly after 8

or 9 p.m. In fact it is stretching a point to say that we have any fast-food businesses at all. There is a fish-and-chip van on St Mary's, and Pom Ellis runs a Thai takeaway, but both are better described for their quality than their speed. They both pack up before dark and so, as far as food for drunks goes, the choice is peanuts or pork scratchings from behind the bar, or nothing.

Believe me, there is no going to sleep for a police officer on St Mary's, knowing there are six homeless inebriates trudging up and down Hugh Street, pointlessly trying to find a kebab shop. Our only option, when we know there is a stag party on the island, is to keep the participants from getting themselves into trouble. Cast a caring eye over them, and every so often drop them a hint about the 3.30 p.m. check-in deadline for the ferry. Once the captain of the *Scillonian III* has slipped his moorings, he ain't coming back for nobody – not even his granny. Leaving without six partially dressed Beach Boys troubles the captain not one jot. Furthermore, he has a set of standards of behaviour, below which he has the right to refuse passage to anyone he doesn't want to take. Being a disorderly drunk falls below these standards.

I see my job as self-appointed mother to the stag parties, for their own well-being. It is crucial to strike up a trusted working relationship with them early in the day. This is where, perhaps, a bit of new legislation would assist this dynamic. I have observed that there does seem to be a pattern to their group behaviour that, were parliament minded to, could be legislated for. For a small consultancy fee I'll offer to draft the entirety of the Stag-Do Act 2016 but as a taster I'll give our government a little bit of it.

Section 4, Sub-section 2A of the Stag-Do Act 2016 arose out of a trying meeting I had on Porthcressa beach several years ago, with a man from St Just called Ben.

My proposed Act will go on to stipulate that: 'Amongst the participants of any stag-do, there must be one reveller – not being the groom – who is the person the rest of the group can consider to be the LIABILITY.'

This person will be the self-appointed Stag-Do Police Liaison Officer. He carries a veto over every other member of the group, and must possess exceptional levels of resilience in the face of the rest of the group saying things like 'Just keep quiet' and 'You're not helping the situation'. This stag must be the one with the loudest voice and richest vocabulary, which can be heard in Dolby-sound quality at a distance of 300 yards – or the length of the beach they are drinking on and playing frisbee, to the annoyance of sunbathers. At any one time, he must be the drunkest person amongst the group by a factor of five.

This skilled negotiator's role is to complain bitterly that he is being spoken to by 'Mr Policeman', and yet refuse to break off the conversation and go away until his twenty-fifth needless apology has been acknowledged with a handshake. An Accomplished Stag Liability is identifiable by the complexity of the handshake he insists on performing. This may include a bump of the knuckles, followed by a triple thumb-grab and clenched fist-to-the-chest love-hold, as if meeting one's homie from the Bronx.

I do try to keep it good-humoured despite the very best efforts of the obligatory 'Liability'. On this occasion Ben was bundled onto the ferry home by his mates without further complication.

In dealing with stag parties I have also had occasion to happen upon the main man, left half naked and alone in the middle of the night, cellophaned to a lamp post along the Strand. I have even had the privilege of being an invited guest at the stag-do of a local man whom we had taken to court only days before. Not every prosecution leaves an irreparably damaged relationship between the police and the defendant.

Once in a while a stag party escapes our notice until much later in the day. These ones become quite complex to manage, as generally all members of the party have reached – and exceeded – the tipping point of comprehension. The 3.30 p.m. check-in deadline is an abstract concept, especially if you have no watch, or indeed trousers, shirt, pants or any clothing at all, for that matter.

I am relieved to say that, to my knowledge, only one stag has chosen to strip completely naked in the middle of the day. So here he is. A call direct to the police-station local number, from a resident mid-afternoon on a Thursday, alerted me to an incident of immediate concern. The caller reported that a man was standing as nature intended, but as the law had regulated against, in Hugh Street in full view of onlookers. There were others, evidently in his party, in Hawaiian shirts, jeering and taking pictures of him. It didn't take a long-in-service officer to realise this was something needing greater exploration, and the description of the attire hinted at it having something to do with a less-than-teetotal pre-wedding event. Already tooled up with radio, stab-jacket and cuffs, and having just finished briefing for the changeover of shifts with PC Nic Gould, who was coming on-duty for the late turn, I departed from the station with him and we hoofed it at a trot down Garrison Lane, past the Wesleyan Chapel to the junction outside Mumford's newsagents.

We were in time to see the Pacific Island fashion-shoot still in progress. Immediately apparent, standing in the middle of the road, was the glamour photographer of the group, directing the action. Clearly possessing a very sophisticated camera app on his smartphone, which could allow for the random camera-sway that comes with ten pints of guest bitter, the photographer was shouting instructions to the model, regarding his pose and poise. The cameraman's able assistants – also recognisable in garish shirts – were standing behind him out of shot, and likewise cat-calling to the supermodel, who was centre-stage ten yards away, fetchingly pressing his bare buttocks up against the window of the 49 Degrees clothes shop to steady himself. He and his nether-regions were facing into the road. He was holding his cheap tropical-green grass skirt in his outstretched right hand and his pants and T-shirt in his left, like he was having an epiphany or had won a boxing bout. For decency's sake, the six-foot one-inch model had left his flip-flops on, along with a fetching garland of plastic flowers in his hair. He had gone to considerable effort to get noticed, to ensure that he would get to the police station – I'll credit him with that.

Onlookers were in abundance at this time of day, and in fact the street was full of people. It was alive with shoppers and visitors, and in amongst it a drunken last hurrah was under way. Stoically the model was being ignored by most passers-by, who recognised this for what it was and did not want to spare the time to imagine his hangover the next day. I fancied that, if I had chanced to look into the window of the deli as I passed at my purposeful stride, I would have seen customers scrabbling for their smartphones and frantically typing in wi-fi codes to enable uploads to their YouTube accounts, in anticipation of the Police v. Naked Man spectacle that was about to unfold.

As a police officer, you just never know how such an encounter with a beer-fortified groom in his birthday suit is going to play out. It is almost always the groom who is involved in this act of theatrics, and none of the remainder of his party. It is a rite of passage. No other member of the entourage can, or should, claim this centre-stage privilege on a stag-do. To upstage the groom is bad form. Far better to let the main man manage the heat with the Old Bill, if it comes to it, for a better chance of a sympathetic outcome.

The intricacies of stag- and hen-dos on Scilly are further complicated by our geography. A stag-do that gets out of hand is most likely to occur in a group on a ferry day-trip from the mainland. Local stags are unlikely to become involved with the police, unless they travel away from the islands to strange lands like Newquay or Penzance. Locals have all been drunk on Scilly on numerous occasions, and yet another binge-drinking event in the same pubs with the same beers, same onlookers and frequently the same ridiculous dress code rarely results in anything more than the same pattern of behaviour, ending in the same stumble home along the same lanes of St Mary's in the same pitch-black. Several times, the most tired and emotional of local stags have been driven home with our blessings in Cop Cabs. Stags from the mainland are a different matter, and their progression from arrival on the boat pre-loaded with lager at midday to leaving at 4 p.m. rarely goes unnoticed by the police. Curiously, hen-dos are almost the polar opposite. It is the local ones, with their pink lists, that come to the notice of police, and the mainland ones largely take place under the radar. I suspect it is a confidence thing. Girls are most happy to play up in front of a home crowd, whereas boys need the cover of anonymity to really let their skirts down.

It was self-evident how Nic and I needed to manage our hot Hawaiian date – decisively, in the circumstances. At 1 a.m. time is not of the essence, and it is often possible to enter into a reasoned conversation with a naked man at night, resulting in a flea in the ear before his inevitable retreat home. In full daylight at 3 p.m., with an audience and a posse of drunk chaperons with a pressing need to board the only ferry back to the mainland before 4 p.m. *with* the groom, there were several factors in play. Neither I nor Nic wanted this to end in an unedifying scrap, with private body-parts offputtingly close to our own flesh – been there, done that, and I never want to go there again. My plan was to stride up to Hawaii-Five-No and get him clear of the busy street, before I made it to stardom on a down-loaded viral video-feature on the Internet.

Seeing me coming from across the road, the groom turned his back on me and lowered his arms, partially as the result of a moment of clarity to hide his John Thomas, and partly as an anthropomorphic gesture to look more diminutive and to show that he was not a threat to the oncoming silverback in the black Kevlar. In the background I could hear the onlookers, both inside and outside the deli, unconsciously doing the 'Wooooooooooooa!' that a good-humoured test-match crowd chants as the fast bowler approaches the crease. This hail has been successfully adapted to include police heading towards comedic imminent arrests, probably born of the same good-humoured crowd entertaining themselves between play watching streakers at Lord's.

Reaching my submissive target, I took hold of his right arm, which was holding the green grass skirt, and arrested him then and there for being naked in public and drunk, followed by the stern words of the Caution. I did not know the man and we had never met before, so it came as a surprise and not a little relief when his immediate words after being cautioned were, 'Are you that copper that does the blog on Facebook? Whatever happens here, keep it up, mate.'

There was no mistaking the code implied in his unsolicited comment. It meant: *I ain't a threat; you are just doing your job, and right now I am a willing and passive part of that task.* I was relieved. I handcuffed him with his hands behind his back and, holding his upper arm so as to support him if he stumbled, walked him across the road to Garrison Lane, which although just ten yards away was marginally more out of public view than the centre of town. As I walked him full-frontal past the picture window of the deli, I used my custodian helmet to protect his modesty. He was, after all, still very much naked.

Nic, in the meantime, was behind me, managing the increasingly tense objections of colourfully shirted members of the groom's fashion-shoot. What was meant to have been a simple striptease in front of men, women and children in a busy high street, with no further consequences, before boarding the *Scillonian III* ferry was not going to plan. Damn the police and their diligence! Why were they there when you didn't want them? Why couldn't they just stick to the accepted format of never being around when you needed them? Nic's negotiator job was the difficult one, although mine became complex when I realised that a man cuffed to the rear does not possess the dexterity to put on his own underpants. Parent-like, I helped him into his boxer shorts, while Nic made friends and influenced people behind me.

Without speaking, we both knew what our plan was next. It distinctly did not involve booking Hawaiian man into custody, followed by a couple of hours' listening to him snore it off in Cell 1, then issuing him with an £80 fine for being Drunk and Disorderly, before turfing him out onto the streets of St Mary's. Alone and penniless, in the early evening, dressed only in flip-flops, pants, a plastic green grass skirt and flowers in his hair, having missed his only boat back home, it was not an option we wanted to engineer for our man. We resolved to take him up the road a short distance towards the police station, issue the fixed-penalty notice, tuck it into the waistband of his skirt and direct him down to the quay to board the boat back to Penzance with his fellow revellers. The law allowed for this solution, so it really wasn't cutting corners, and for an otherwise-agreeable chap it was an option that would see him home and smoothing it all over with his fiancée by dark.

All three of us were amenable to that plan, so we put it in motion. Nic had gained the trust of the remainder of the group and, with that trust, came thirst, so they temporarily forgot about the groom and went off to another pub to Facebook each other – and the world – the events of the afternoon, over pint eleven.

Hawaii Five-No left us where we were standing, just outside the police station, and shimmied his way on, to rendezvous with the rest of his group for fortification before the journey home. Nic and I headed down to the quay, where passengers were gathering to board the ferry that was due to depart at 4.15. Outwardly it would appear that our job was done, but the gig ain't over for us on Scilly until the fat lady sails . . . with its cargo. Two risks still existed. Risk 1: the Hawaiian party misses the boat. Risk 2: the captain of the *Scillonian* refuses to offer them passage back to the mainland.

The safety and comfort of the ferry passengers and crew are well accepted as the primary concern of the captain, and it is always his right to refuse passage, no matter how complex that leaves matters on Scilly. We fully respect that, even though it is a point that means the castaways remain our problem. It is a common misconception, or local belief, that the police have some power to export troublemakers from the islands. The Wild West equivalent of running the villain out to the county-line and telling him not to come back, unless he wants to face the rope. There is no more truth in this on Scilly than in any place in the UK, but never let that get in the way of expectations. This and countless previous occasions would be seen as an 'export', no matter how distant we kept ourselves from the actual departure.

It was, for Nic and me, a tense game of brinkmanship. Overcoming Risk 1 required us to diplomatically remind the distracted party that the boat was about to leave, without further exciting them or giving them any cause to become disorderly. Overcoming Risk 2 required us to stay sufficiently in the background for the captain not to get concerned that an 'export' was under way. If the stag party got leery or played up, Nic and I would be stuck with them all night and that was a dreary prospect.

This particular group, however, was either superbly managed by us or more probably just a decent bunch of chaps, who saw the naked photo-shoot and subsequent fine as the perfect dramatic end to a bachelor life for their friend. As they calmly passed Nic and me on the quay, a nervously short time before any further boarding was halted, I thanked the groom for his respectful demeanour; and one of them, presumably the best man, quipped that I had fined his friend by the inch. A factor that, as he said it, was destined to be played out with embellishment in the wedding speech in due course. Better that than in court, in this circumstance.

The captain allowed them passage. The horn of the ship was sounded and she pulled out of St Mary's harbour. I later heard that the skill of a mariner of many years ensured that the motion of the ship gently rocked the stag party to a passive beery slumber all the way back to Penzance.

THE WINGS OF
ACHILLES

I learnt all about my Achilles heel in the spring of 2012. The consultant who taught me about it showed me on the X-ray where it could be found, and where the tendon that connected it to the calf muscle of my right leg had snapped.

Many men in their mid-forties think they are still young. Relatively speaking, they are, but let's be honest: Olympic events with sportsmen over the age of thirty-five are somewhat more pedestrian competitions, with less TV coverage. These types of men – and I count myself in their number – forget we are no longer twenty-four years old, simply because the sports shops we go to have trained their staff not to snigger at us. Forty-plus blokes have wondrous things like mortgages, careers and an increasing number of trousers in the wardrobe that shrink at the waist if not worn for six months. To help us forget this collection of responsibilities and phenomena, a goodly number of us hark back to our mid-twenties and simpler times, when our physicality knew no bounds.

We take up sports and fitness regimes that nature never intended for the species, at any age. Sports like squash and badminton, for instance, which were without a doubt, in my mind, invented by cardiovascular surgeons on the make. I suppose, however, these racket sports could vaguely be thought to appeal to some vestige of basic human evolution. Chasing a ball around must mimic hunting prey: small birds or fast butterflies, perhaps. Circuit training, on the other hand, was invented by orthopaedic surgeons trying to get in on the act. This exercise regime has no obvious link to evolution. It is punishment for punishment's sake. The body is not designed for such absurd movement. It is just a succession of ridiculous hops, jumps, pushes and skips that serves no purpose other than to exhaust, induce swearing and break skeleton and muscle. No pain, no financial gain – for surgeons anyway.

In 2012 I was big into circuit training. The sports teacher at Five Islands School, Martin 'Songy' Songhurst, devised his own evening torture routine for us grown-ups. He inflicted it weekly on gullible volunteers on a Wednesday evening at the new Queen Elizabeth II Sports Hall.

As an aside, and should it be necessary for identification reasons, other than PC Mat Crowe, Songy is the only other man on Scilly who resolutely insists on dressing inappropriately for all seasons. He is in a permanent state of sports awareness. As the tennis coach and PE teacher at the school, his plumage never changes, other than by a Nike tick or a Slazenger slash. Kitted out entirely in sportswear and more often than not carrying a tennis racket, he is a tennis fanatic always on the ready to return a volley, should it come his way, night or day: on the court, in the pubs or out and about around town. I have never seen him without shorts on. Every day of the week, every week of the year and in every state of weather, from the scorching sun to force-ten gales, Songy wears his white Umbro tennis shorts and trainers. Some say he is sponsored by a cartel of renegade orthopaedic surgeons in West Cornwall. I won't hear of this, as I have little doubt he is a man of great integrity who simply owns no trousers; or perhaps none of the trousers in his wardrobe fit.

Each Wednesday evening I happily went along to Songy's circuit-training class, to give other over-forties men something to aspire to. The exertion levels that Songy put us to gave me the opportunity to practise new profanities, which I had learnt from working on the street the week before. It also neatly dovetailed with my need to keep fit. The Home Office was bringing in a mandatory fitness test for all police at the time. I knew I had to get fit or risk losing my job.

The weekly training session consisted of about ten exercise stations, each with a different cruel and inhumane torture. The object was to self-inflict each punishment for thirty seconds apiece, before moving on to the next. This got around Article 3 of the Human Rights Act (Prohibition of Torture) because it was done voluntarily. There were sit-ups, squats, push-ups, weights and a vaulting horse. At the last we had to bounce over the top and back again as many times as possible, presumably (in my case) in readiness for jumping over garden fences while pursuing a suspect.

Songy timed us and blew his whistle, so that we knew when to move on to the next exercise. By the time

I got to the vaulting horse I was pretty much warmed up. Some onlookers would say 'knackered'. A few enthusiastic bounces later and I heard a massive 'CRACK!', as if somebody had slapped me with a cricket bat on the calf. I looked round to see who had hit me, but nobody was there. Then I fell over, because only one of my legs worked, and the stars I could see when I put my right leg on the ground were better viewed from a horizontal position. It hurt, and technically I may have committed a public-order offence with the use of several expletives in a public place.

I knew, without any previous medical knowledge, that I had snapped a tendon in my ankle. The remainder of the group glanced up at me briefly, before noting that I was not clutching my heart having a cardiac arrest, nor was there any blood. I was a casualty that could wait. All told, I lay there for forty-five minutes while the rest of the session continued, before somebody kindly drove me to the hospital.

The locum doctor looked at me. 'You've torn a muscle. Go home and rest it. Here are some crutches.'

On that occasion, and rarely for the excellent doctors over here, the initial diagnosis was not on the mark. I hobbled back and forth to work on crutches for four days. I abandoned any prospect of foot patrol and stayed in the office. By the third day I took myself back to hospital for a second opinion. This time I was given the prescription I needed: a voucher for a subsidised flight to the mainland to West Cornwall Hospital in Penzance.

The hospital we have on Scilly is brilliant. The nurses and doctors are great, and friendly, and anyone who has any involvement with the health provision here really does put the word 'care' into healthcare. There are limitations, however. There is no full Accident & Emergency department. Operations cannot be performed here. All casualties with life-threatening conditions have to go directly to the mainland.

To get there, helicopter services provide this vital link for us, day and night. During daylight hours, when the weather permits, the Cornwall Air Ambulance does the trip. At night or in rough weather the Royal Navy or, latterly, Bristow's provides the search-and-rescue capability. However, my voucher was not for a trip on one of these choppers. I was lucky enough to get one of the commercial helicopter flights out of Scilly, while it still operated here. The Sikorsky S-61is the civil variant of the Sea King helicopter. It's built to get you to your destination, through rough or smooth. It is the plane that takes oil-rig workers out to the platforms in the North Sea. It is not built for luxury.

The commercial passenger service to St Mary's from Cornwall flew for forty-eight years, up till October 2012. It was far and away the most popular way to travel to Scilly for the annual holiday. Some seem to consider its demise as they would that of an old friend. I would agree that it was fun to travel on. It felt a bit like you were going to war. It was incredibly loud and juddery. As it lifted off, it used to rattle the teeth in my head as if it were under fire from, and returning fire to, the Vietcong. You never forget the smell and feel of the exhaust fumes, as the helicopter vents partially burnt aviation fuel down the side of the chopper into your face, as you climb the steps to board, with the rotor blades whirring manically, seemingly only inches above your head.

The cabin attendant would see you to your seat and then pointlessly shout at you, at the top of their voice, from two feet away, but the noise from the rotors drowned them out completely, save for a few salient words. From that partially heard message you had to presume that you had gleaned their meaning. I just know that if it had been my job, I would have taken to shouting anything to the passengers, safe in the knowledge that all but expert lip-readers would have only the faintest idea of what I said. 'I said your luck has run out. Your LIFEJACKET is missing from UNDER YOUR SEAT. You must SIT HERE with the broken SEATBELT.' Vertical take-off is strange, too, as is the bit when the pilot flies the helicopter backwards for twenty feet, before slamming into forward and swooping away from the airfield to 1,500 feet. Every bit of the ride was either exhilarating or terrifying, and always memorable. I think it was so loved by visitors because subconsciously it felt like they were being airlifted out of their year-long war zone to a week or two of R&R in a safe allied territory.

My dear friend and colleague Adam Cornish will hate me for committing this to paper, but I feel a short story helps to provide an example of how the prospect of a ride in a Sikorsky S-61 is such an exciting one that it clouds all reason. I joined the police service after Adam, in 1995. Joining then meant that, as the most junior on section, I had to make the tea. In the event, I remained the most junior for eighteen months and so skivvied for the team of police officers for a year and a half. I pledged to even things up.

On my first stint to Scilly, Adam asked to come out and visit me one summer. I phoned him and offered to get him the tickets for the helicopter, as they would be easier for me to obtain. They weren't cheap – in fact, mile for mile, I am told it was the most expensive commercial flight in the world. At that time it was cheaper to fly to New York from Gatwick. Adam winced when I told him the price. Well, he would, I suppose, because I exaggerated. I then told him I could get him a cheaper price (the real price) because he was a serving police officer, but that it came with a certain stipulation. If he wanted to knock down the price, he had to travel aboard as if he were one of the flying crew to make up numbers, in a full immersion suit.

I could tell Adam wasn't convinced and didn't know where to get such a suit in any event. I told him that our stores department at Headquarters, where he was, loaned them out all the time and were well aware of this arrangement. After he rang off, I hastily rang the stores and told them of the ruse. Of course they had no such thing as an off-the-peg diver's immersion suit. I knew that, so I asked them, if Adam came in, to confirm to him that a wetsuit would suffice, under their accord with the helicopter company and Civil Aviation rules. At considerable boost to my morale, the lady at the front desk there agreed to my ruse and she must have pulled a blinder because, several weeks later, Adam arrived on the chopper in his wetsuit, albeit with his clothes over the top. He didn't want to look daft.

We laugh about it now: how I duped him into togging up like a scuba diver, sweating profusely under four millimetres of neoprene, on a hot July day on a commercial passenger flight. I say we laugh about it now, but really my laughter is nervous, for Adam's an inspector now and outranks me, so my telling of this story is potentially career-limiting. Jolly good chap, he is. I only wish I might get the opportunity to make him tea for another eighteen months.

Leaving aside my rapidly vanishing job prospects, and going back to my potentially disabling leg injury, I took my NHS flight voucher and secured a seat the very next day to Penzance Heliport. The crossing was unremarkable, but for the fact that it was a remarkable form of transport. I disembarked at Penzance where, beyond the call of duty, stood Inspector Phillips. I hobbled over to her like Tiny Tim and gave her a wan smile. 'Err, I think I've buggered my leg, Ma'am.' She never showed it, but I am sure she must have been concerned about how I was going to effectively police Scilly for the next six months while my injury healed.

And so it was that one Thursday in early April I found myself in the men's Weekend Warrior Ward of the Royal Cornwall Hospital, alongside guys all about my age, all with tales of sporting woe.

The surgeon came to my bedside. 'Hmm, I see from the X-ray that you have full separation of the Achilles tendon in your right leg, Mr . . . Taylor.' He was looking at my papers on the clipboard at the end of my bed.

'Is that bad?' I responded.

Consultants are uninterested in such questioning, in much the same way as I, in interviews, am uninterested in answering questions posed by the suspect. The consultant was clearly not going to get chit-chatty with this patient. He moved on with his interrogation of me.

'Hmm. How did you do it?'

'Jumping repeatedly over a vaulting horse for thirty seconds. I heard it snap with a bang, I fell over and then I started to swear heavily.'

'Hmm. Did you warm up first?'

'Yes. It had been a stressful day. I had been cursing under my breath all afternoon.'

'Hmm. You'll need an operation. It is the bank holiday weekend. Can you come back on Tuesday?'

'Not really. I live on Scilly. I flew over this morning and have just hitch-hiked on crutches the forty miles to this hospital. I haven't anywhere to go tonight, or any way of getting home.'

'Hmm. I'll see what I can do.'

He moved on to the next sad gladiator in the bed beside me, on his way around the ward, prioritising who to operate on that day. I overheard equally compelling tales of hardship from all of the beds' occupants.

Surgeons specialising in foot- and leg-surgery may be aloof, but that is because they are battle-hardened by war stories from weekend warriors like me. My consultant, Mr Butler, in particular – literally. For much of the year he gave up his time to operate on soldiers suffering terrible wounds in Afghanistan and Iraq. I couldn't have been in better hands. Half an hour later, he came back to the ward and broke the news to some that they would have to hobble home for the bank holiday. He elected to operate on me the very next day. My only fear then was what would be expected of me, once I had recovered from one of his battlefield operations. Would I be thought less of, if I didn't hike across the Arctic tundra, row the Pacific or win a medal at the Paralympics, like the armed-services heroes he had patched up over the years?

A successful operation and a few days later, I was discharged from hospital. Inspector Phillips had visited my bedside and brought me grapes. They were genuinely meant, and a touching gesture, but underlying that was an unspoken message we both understood: 'These are magic grapes. You must get better quickly or you will be off the rock.'

There is pragmatically no room for a prolonged period of sickness for police officers on Scilly. It is impractical to keep dispatching mainland officers to the archipelago to back-fill, and the remaining fit officers are therefore duty-bound to take up the slack and fill in for the out-of-commission officer. I was very fortunate in that I worked with two superb constables at the time, PC Mat Collier and PC Marc Blyth. They both stepped up to the mark and, without complaint, dug in to cover the shifts and duties I was unable to fulfil. I remain very grateful to them both.

I returned to Scilly to convalesce, but living so close to the police station, this meant that in practice I went to work. While Mat and Marc covered the shifts and duties I couldn't do, I busied myself with the paperwork and, incrementally, on-crutches patrol, too. Six months later I was back on two feet doing my normal duties. I even returned to circuit training.

I have now raised 'Songy' to target status, and there is a bounty on his head. In due course I intend to bring him to The Hague, for offences against humanity. That's if I can catch him. He is still quick on his toes.

PROFICIENT CYCLING

I passed my Cycling Proficiency Test in the autumn of 1976. Only two of us were on the course: me and another boy my age, eleven, also from a forces family. The trainer took both of us out onto the runways at Biggin Hill RAF base, where I was living with my mum and dad at the time. I can remember the big, wide, flat expanses of tarmac that we had to pretend were roads, and where during the war heroes had become airborne in iconic planes. We used the airbase on a Sunday when there was no flying, cycling around the quiet Nissen huts and hangars to learn the skills that would keep us alive on real roads. Our trainer drew the junctions on the runways with white chalk, for us to practise and observe. There were no such frills as helmets or fluorescent jackets in those days. We took our own bikes and wore shorts and T-shirts.

My push-bike was nothing special – an unbranded model that looked just like one a child would draw. Correction, it looked just like a bike I would still draw, for I do not profess to have any artistic abilities with a pencil. It had two identical-sized wheels, a seat and handlebars. It was

---

gold, I think, and no covetable make or model. I liked it because it was very stable and I had learnt to ride no-handed. I did, however, envy the other boy's bike. He had a dark-red Raleigh Chopper, the bike on every Christmas wish-list in those years. It is still a cult bike of fond renown today, with its distinctive big rear wheel and little front wheel, but is no longer in production. Every cool kid had one. My fellow trainee was that cool kid.

We were instructed in techniques such as approaching the junction, mounting, dismounting and safe braking. This part we both sailed through, and our instructor was happy with our progress. Then came signalling – the bit where your hand has to leave the handlebars. We started off with a left-hand turn. Cycle on the left, turn left: an easy manoeuvre. Naturally it involved looking behind, slowing for the junction and signalling with the left arm held straight out horizontally, while keeping your balance with the right hand on the handlebars. I managed this easily, as did the cool kid, although like any rider of a Chopper, he was less confident at riding one-handed. Such a wicked bike, but it loses some of its magic when you are not in full control of both handles. You see, the problem with the Raleigh Chopper is that although it is uber-cool, it is also uber-unstable. The little wheel at the front acts just like the anarchist wheels on the last shopping trolley in the supermarket car park. For similar reasons that a Tyrannosaurus rex, with its tiny front arms, could not have changed a duvet, a Raleigh Chopper cannot steer a straight line. Both hands are necessary on the handlebars just to stabilise that sucker, because of its small front wheel. Add to that applying the front brake without simultaneously applying the rear, and only the bus-driving skills of Sandra Bullock are going to control a Raleigh Chopper without ending in a trip over the handlebars.

My right-hand turn was very smooth and balanced. Look behind, signal, slow down and turn. The cool kid had to remove his right hand from his rear brake. He wobbled when he slowed with the front brake, and in a panic removed his left hand from the handlebars and crossed it over to grab the right handle. This is an impossible move, even for the most accomplished clown, especially on a Raleigh Chopper. As if in slow motion, he went into a chaotic wobble that he was never going to pull out of. To save himself from falling to the side and grazing his knees, he put his right hand back down onto his left handlebar. His arms were now crossed in front of him. His brain must have been in spasm, trying to figure out which hand operated which brake and how to pull out of an inevitable crash. He applied the front brake instead of the rear and pitched over the handlebars onto the runway. For the first time in thirty-one years another pilot went airborne from an iconic piece of transporting history. His Cycling Proficiency Test was over, and I suspect his Raleigh Chopper lost some of its allure. It certainly did for me. I finished the course and still have both my badge to prove it, and the skin on my palms.

As a reward for passing my cycle test, my parents bought me a road bike with a larger frame and bigger wheels, and I never rode a child's bike again until Isaac lent me his, in May 2014.

May is the most vibrant month on Scilly. The visitors have returned and the season has properly got under way. Everyone is busy and everything is fresh and exciting. Mike

Nelhams, the head gardener, and his team have nurtured the beautiful Tresco Abbey Garden into a riot of colour. Gangs of red squirrels that include Mike's postcode in their territory are, to his relief, weaning themselves off his succulent pink protea heads and back onto easy street, mugging visitors for rocky-road bars and flapjacks at the garden café instead.

Tripper boats that had been hauled out of the water in the autumn are all spruced up. The winter saw their deck boards lifted, to reveal the bounty in the oily filth of the sump water. This is where the pound coins that fell from the clumsy hands and pockets of passengers ended up. They rolled through the gaps in the nailed-down flooring into the unreachable bilges, to form a sterling ballast. Once retrieved, they are laundered in the quiet nights of January, February and March through the local pub tills, with purchases of Tribute, Betty Stogs or Proper Job ales. The boards are then sanded down and carefully nailed back in place, with precision gaps calculated to filter out foreign currency. The boats themselves have been freshly painted in their familiar colours of yellow, blue, green and red, to tempt hapless, clumsy landlubbers on board. Back in the water, they set to shuttling hundreds of people back and forth from one island to the next, bouncing them about, to rattle the change from their clutches. Carefully calculated to distract them, the skippers announce safety briefings with dry advice to passengers: 'Exit the boat to port onto the quay if you enjoyed the journey, and to starboard into the sea if you didn't.'

Cafés on all the islands are open, with fresh menus announcing a hundred different ways to suspend any notion of dieting. New waiting staff are finding it easy to tempt people off the bathroom scales with irresistible mackerel pâté, salads of crab and lobster caught in pots within sight of their table, and locally netted megrim and John Dory. Avifauna with chicks on nests and a fresh set of plumage are charming al-fresco diners, distracting them to the left while others sneak in to steal morsels from the right. So much crime abounds, and yet so little of it is reported, let alone investigated.

The planes are all flying and the *Scillonian* is sailing six days a week. It is all busy with the potential energy of a fresh battery. The World Pilot Gig Championships are out of the way by now, and the excitement of a summer patrolling by and on the sea lies ahead. Almost everyone is in good humour, with a bounce in their stride. On a sunny day I can imagine no better place to be on the beat. It is a great time of year to police Scilly.

With much enthusiasm, I booked on-duty at 8 a.m. on a glorious morning in May. It was just me on-duty that morning, with Mat due on later at 4 p.m. for the evening shift. I looked at the list I had pinned on the wall: the one I scribbled out and stuck above the computer, to remind us all of the various different housekeeping tasks we should complete at the start of each shift. Little tasks to make sure we have covered all the bases. It is basically our way of self-briefing for the day ahead. Unlike many police stations on the mainland, we do not benefit from a scripted briefing, with lists of stolen vehicles and pictures of the latest newly released convict who is suspected of becoming criminally active again. There is no canteen we can gather in to trade war-stories or share information. We mostly work alone.

Sometimes we may not even see each other from one week to the next, if the changeover between shifts doesn't coincide. It can be quite a lonely vigil on occasion. We are labelled as Neighbourhood Officers, but the necessity of being omni-competent means that we are involved in pretty much every policing discipline. One minute we are Neighbourhood Officers, the next acting as CID or Traffic, Family Protection Unit or Licensing, Crime Scene Investigators or Special Branch. It is as varied as the whole of a police force, and because of this, every chief constable who has visited hands back the reins to the sergeant as Chief Constable of Scilly when they leave.

The morning job list is therefore quite long. We have nobody to point out what we have missed. It includes, as a matter of priority, checking for newly reported crime. We average between one and two a week, across the whole of the year. This is really pretty low in the grand scheme of things, making us a beat vying for position to claim the lowest crime rate in the UK. A journalist once wrote a piece on Scilly and charmingly laid claim to it being 'The Land that Crime Forgot'. This was seized upon by the promoters of Scilly and has appeared in brochures and other journalistic pieces ever since. It's probably more accurate to claim that Scilly is 'The Land that Forgot about Crime', but I do accept that this does not have the same ring about it.

The lack of fear of crime out here is palpable. Some visitors I meet seem confused that there are police here at all. I guess, after twenty-one years in the police service, I have grown used to the fact that crime is not created by a geography but by its population. There is no crime on the

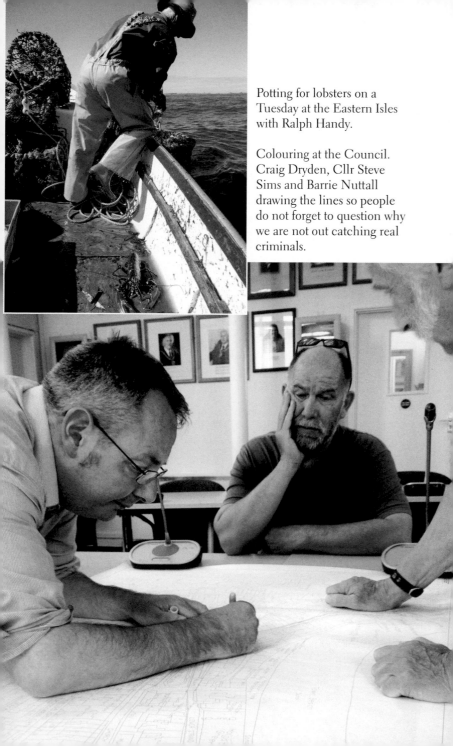

Potting for lobsters on a Tuesday at the Eastern Isles with Ralph Handy.

Colouring at the Council. Craig Dryden, Cllr Steve Sims and Barrie Nuttall drawing the lines so people do not forget to question why we are not out catching real criminals.

Not yellow but primrose in keeping with the area of outstanding natural beauty.

Trying to recoup my losses at both boating and issuing tickets. If I can sell these mackerel at Fortnum & Mason to a billionaire I may break even on this trip.

On sunny days I go to the off islands. On cloudy days I send the others. PC Nic Gould Landing at Carn Near, Tresco.

The punishment for Lewis for not tidying his room was several tides on Bishops Rock. He survived. Therefore guilty.

Leaving so soon Sir? PC Marc Blyth seeing the boat off.

The folly of not reading the small print when taking the job of constable on Scilly. PC Mat Crowe and his shapely legs.

Top left: Deputy Chief Constable Mowgli (retired) AKA Station Cat. He gives the orders, we follow dutifully.

Left: "Oh. Are you the guy who does the Facebook stuff? Whatever happens here keep it up, Mate"
OK. I'll keep it up if you keep your pants up.

At least I have my Elf. Police Constable Mat Collier and Santa in the Grotto.

Mary Winter MBE and myself at Park House Residential Home. She painted cats. Oh! and coded and broadcast the message for the D Day landings at Bletchley Park amongst other things.

Escorting the May Queen and entourage all the way to the Wicker Man.

Every victim counts, even abducted goldfish. PC Mark Jory applying emergency 1st AID at the scene of the crime.

Working with children is vitally important for us. Here they are teaching Mat how to count without having to take his shoes and socks off.

An inspirational place to write. Especially about crime.

island of Samson, for instance. Equally there is no resident population there, either. People everywhere possess frailties and flaws. Scilly is no different, but that doesn't make it less special. In the winter months we can go for several weeks without a specific call to action through the official channels. Yes, weeks. This is what makes going through the morning list pretty important. So we do not miss anything. Sometimes a colleague may have been called out in the night. The first the rest of us may know about it will be during these checks in the morning.

Such must have been the case for the early-turn officer who came on-duty after a night I was called out to a noise complaint.

In my capacity as a new resident of the islands, I was invited to a house party along Church Road. There were members of the community there from the harbour staff, lifeboat, coastguard and many other nautically minded people and their spouses. It was a bit of a boozy affair, but sadly I was on-call, so I could not partake. I stood chatting, while everyone else got increasingly inebriated. My host, the assistant harbour master Bill Burrows, was very attentive and introduced me successively to many people throughout the evening. It became transparently obvious to me, as the evening wore on and as more wine and beer were drunk, just why I had been invited along in the first place. I do not resent the reason even for a second. People just wanted to suss me out, to find out which way I might jump on certain policing issues. Was I a zealot, or was I there to stick my feet up on the desk and eat doughnuts for a couple of years? What they would have cause to fear, and how I might impact on their lives, was clearly the reason for the gathering. I suspected they must have got their heads together beforehand to share out topics they wanted to quiz me on. It was a gentle inquisition, subtle at first in the early, sober part of the evening, when I was gently probed on my stance on things like the wearing of seatbelts.

'So you are the new policeman. What sort of car do you drive? I saw you getting into the police Land Rover earlier today and buckling up. Do you feel that is necessary out here?'

We would then have a five-minute amicable chat about the subject and the questioner would make his or her excuses and deliver the news on my position in hushed tones to the rest of the room. Somebody else would move in with a different topic. It was like tag-wrestling, but with questions. By the end of the evening I was being confronted by the person who had drawn the short straw. The drink-drive question.

'So, hic! Are you going to nick me if I drive my car home tonight? Hic!'

'I'm sure you are only talking hypothetically, aren't you? So of course, in such hypothetical circumstances, then yes I would.'

'Hic! Yes, hypothetical. Hic!'

The evening ended for me shortly before midnight, not because I was fed up, but because I had to be up in the morning for my shift. I actually quite enjoyed the whole evening, even though it had not been quite what I expected.

I went home and straight to bed. Half an hour later the bedside phone rang. It was Comms, asking if I knew where Church Street was and could I go there, as there was a report of a noisy party. I got into my uniform and went back on my own to the gathering I had just left, where I was able to give them an unequivocal understanding of my position regarding noisy parties in the small hours – a question they had rather clumsily omitted to ask me about earlier.

That May morning, there were a few new matters that had come in overnight since my last shift. Checking the answerphone revealed a plea from a fraught visitor, a parent whose child had lost their toy giraffe. I wrote down their contact details, made a note about the state of the vanishing wildlife and deleted the message. The next voice was from a local shop owner, recounting how they had had a giraffe handed over the counter to them. Making a reasonably safe assumption that the two might be linked, I married the two callers up with each other and called back the grateful safari-park ranger.

I never need to check the cells in the morning, to see if there have been any interesting guests brought in over-night. If any prisoners had been arrested after bedtime, anyone in my family trying to sleep above would have heard them. Inevitably this would have gone on to feature as a talking point at breakfast. In addition to this convenient domestic early-warning system, I am the custody officer for all prisoners arrested by anyone in the team. Every time there is an arrest, I get called out – on-duty, off-duty, middle of the night, middle of the day, when I am boating, enter-taining, watching TV, even with my leg in plaster on crutches on one occasion. Between the three of us, we make about twenty arrests a year on Scilly. In the scheme of things, no big commitment really. If it is me making the arrest, I call out one of the other officers to take on the role of being Officer in the Case (OIC). They then take on the detainee and I become the custody officer. In this new role, my main task is to look after the welfare of the detainee, ensure they get their rights, and remain as neutral to the actual investigation as it is possible to be out here. When the detainee is my arrest, I get the other officer to present my own prisoner back to me, for me to consider whether I have lawfully arrested them. I have not turned one down yet.

'So tell me, Officer. Why did I arrest this man?'

'I dunno, Sarge, I wasn't there. You arrested him. I was in bed asleep at the time.'

Happy in the knowledge that there were no prisoners or other pressing matters that morning, I planned some cathartic persecution of motorists for trivial matters, like bald tyres, broken lights, ineffective brakes or no seatbelts, just so that I could give motorists the opportunity to question whether or not I had any real criminals to catch. These are the little matters that are responsible for killing more people than the things that really get people's goat out here. If you want to make an impact as a policeman on Scilly, then address the feeding of gulls or crack down on people talking above sixty decibels after dark in the street at night. That's what animates many people here, and I can't see that changing soon. March around telling people off for things there are no laws about and, in some opinions, you will have done a fine job. Suck on your teeth at a set of tyres with slicks like a Formula 1 racing car, and you are on an officious warpath.

Some years ago PC Marc Blyth received an irate call to the police station about a film crew at Porthcressa beach.

They were causing uproar because of their outrageous behaviour. He slung on his helmet and jacket and headed off on foot to the beach, where he found that a well-known wildlife presenter was doing a piece to camera on the perceived nuisance of gulls stealing food. He was trying to make the point that these incredible animals are just doing what they are hard-wired to do: scavenge. Gulls are marvellous animals, too. Next time you are at the beach, just take a good look at the first herring gull you see. Suspend your learnt revulsion. I am not asking you to consider befriending or cuddling one. I fully accept that gulls have a vicious bill, which looks like it could eviscerate you at a whim; and having handled them many times, that is no idle observation.

For starters, gulls look incredible, with their pure-white head plumage and pale-grey back. Theirs is the sleekness of James Bond in his tuxedo just before the poker game. If gulls wore ties, they would always be straightening the knot to emphasise their perfection. Incredible fliers, because they have to be, they are avian pirates that have evolved to rob the fishy forages from other hard-working seabirds. They harry the smaller birds in flight until they regurgitate their meal, or scavenge from the dead or dying of the sea. Think of gulls as Revenue & Customs – tax collectors of the ocean. It is what they did for millions of years, until we came along and hoovered up the large shoals of fish and depleted the smaller birds through the loss of their habitats. These resourceful birds saw egg-and-cress sandwiches and ice-cream cones as fair compensation for herring. And this food source came with an even dumber victim to rob, too – one who holds the edible bounty in full sight or gives it to their young ones, who are even less wary. Better still, on occasion these humans actually throw the morsels at gulls. What's not to like? Given another million years, at the rate we are going, gulls will have fully adapted to stealing off us. No more a 'herring gull', but more of a 'cod and chips gull'.

Perhaps drawing a comparison with tax collectors may not have endeared you to the herring gull. Clearly Marc's irate phone caller was not going to be easily persuaded into loving gulls. Five feet from a sign saying DON'T FEED THE GULLS, Marc watched the presenter offering up a newspaper wrapping of chips to the birds gathering around him. Behind him, Marc's informant was incandescent with rage. These terse little signs, like DON'T FEED THE GULLS, KEEP OFF THE GRASS, NO BALL GAMES, have no lawful meaning. They are erected without any regard for how they can ever be enforced. The thing is that once a sign is up, it gives the appearance of having some legal backing to it. 'No Ball Games' is a great one, along with 'No Parking in Front of This Garage'.

What could Marc do? The presenter was reinforcing a point that would increase the prejudice. Marc approached the film crew and made the point that feeding the birds was not increasing the presenter's fan-base – a point that failed to gain traction. No amount of emotional appeal could get the presenter to reconsider his editorial piece. He knew his rights, and Marc duly retreated, before drawing a crowd. The show got its shot.

If we have enquiries to do on other islands that are not urgent, we truck down to the quay to purchase a ticket for the tripper boats, like everyone else. These boats generally leave the quay between 10 and 10.15, to return at midday and later in the afternoon. Once we commit to going to an off-island, we are there until we can catch the next boat back. The sensible solution most of the time is to store up a bundle of enquiries for each island. A simple trip for a shotgun licence-check that may take thirty minutes leaves us filling the remaining four hours, until the boat returns, with a pleasant foot patrol. These are the moments when we are beholden to the boats for the majority of our transport needs around the archipelago.

At 9.45 a.m. on the glorious May morning, I received a phone call direct to our police-station phone. The caller on the other end spoke in urgent, hushed tones, as I imagined a member of the French Resistance would behind enemy lines. I didn't press them when they indicated that they didn't want to tell me who they were. This was a secret agent, deep undercover, after all. In reality I didn't need to press them. I recognised the voice, and they probably knew that, but it was a bit of mutual subterfuge and an irrelevance, so we moved on to the meat of the call. The secret agent told me there was a person they were concerned about, drink-driving on a quad bike on the roads on the island of Bryher. The caller gave me enough detail to figure out that there was a fair-to-middling chance of catching them over the limit, if I managed to get out there within the hour. This was going to need swift action. No time, or necessity at that stage, to call Mat on-duty early. I'd do this one myself. I thanked the caller and hung up.

I had a decent chance of catching the culprit. Bryher was just two miles away, a twenty-minute journey by boat.

There was no capacity to take the Land Rover, so I would have to be on foot once I was away from St Mary's. Collecting a fluorescent breathalyser box, I hot-footed it down to the harbour, to see who might be going across to the other islands.

Joe Badcock, on his light-blue boat *Guiding Star*, was just about to cast off. I shouted down to him, over the heads of the passengers that he already had aboard, 'You going to Bryher, Joe?'

'No, sorry, Col. The tide is out. There's no water to get down the channel until three p.m. I can drop you at Carn Near on Tresco – you could hitch across to Bryher, if you can find a smaller boat – if that's any good to you.'

'OK, coming aboard. Everyone here got their vaccination certificates?'

I hopped on and muscled my way to the front of the boat, through the ranks of Gortex-robed old hands and naïve, T-shirt-wearing newbie passengers.

I took a seat just across from a young lad and his mother, and we set off. The young man was about eleven years old and kept me under close observation for the first half of the journey. There was something about the way he was looking at me, in deep thought with his head tilted slightly to one side, that made me feel he was not about to ask the usual childlike questions. Things like 'How many murderers have you arrested?', 'Have you got a gun?' and 'What's inside your hat?'

He was evidently thinking about my mission, which had been declared in my announcement to Joe. My plight was that I needed to get to Bryher from Tresco. From where we were due to land, it would be more than a mile-and-a-half speed-walking in the heat, in full uniform, to a different quay at New Grimsby. From there I would have to sit in the sunshine, swinging my legs over the edge of the quay and playing the waiting game. After seeing if anyone was about, I could then cadge a lift for the 400-yard hop across to Bryher.

Out of the blue, the boy chirped up quite matter-of-factly, 'Do you want to borrow my bike? I have one at Carn Near, leaning against the rocks at the top of the quay. You can leave it at New Grimsby, and Mum and I will pick it up there later.'

I looked at his mum. She shrugged. 'If it's all right by Isaac, it is all right by me.'

I chatted with the future logistics expert for the remainder of the short journey and learnt that he was on his annual Scilly holiday with his parents. He knew the islands better than I did. It clearly didn't concern him what my urgency was all about. He was just helping out a policeman in a tight spot.

When we got to Carn Near, I thanked Isaac and made my way up the quay to where he had hidden his bike. Of course I should have expected as much, but there was a child's bike with a child-sized frame. At five-foot ten, I am not exactly lofty, but with all the kit I was wearing and the tall helmet, I was overly massive once I managed to lower myself onto the saddle. I could put both feet flat on the ground with my knees still bent at right-angles. All it lacked on my helmet was a flashing blue light, and I would have been every part the ridiculous Keystone Cop, which would have appealed to everyone's stereotype of me.

I drew a small crowd as I learnt to ride again. Not since

Biggin Hill had I been on a bike this small. Inevitably the cameras emerged from the onlookers' backpacks, as they smirkingly committed to pixels my humiliation. Despite the increasing absurdity of the situation, I was still conscious that there was a potential drink-driver on the roads and I needed to get to him before anyone was harmed. It had now been about forty minutes since I had received the original phone call.

Once I had found my balance I set off, to a ripple of poorly suppressed giggles, and cycled down the narrow concrete road, parallel with the beautiful white sweep of sand at Appletree Bay, which led from the dunes at the southern end of Tresco. Sitting hunched over the child's handlebars, I found that my rigid stab-jacket rode up high under my chin every time my pedals reached the twelve o'clock position. The wind flapped my trousers, and my knees were up around my ears as I pedalled. It was marvellous! On the short downhills I could freewheel and stretch out my legs, to relieve the cramp that was building up. On the uphills I had to dig deep and put my back into it, just to go faster than walking pace. When I came silently up behind walkers, I rang the bell on the handlebars to give them warning that I was coming through. They would turn to see me bearing down on them, and would scatter to the side of the road wide-eyed in disbelief at what they were seeing.

It felt like living. If Enid Blyton had written a book about the policeman that Dick from the Famous Five would grow up to be, I could not have been a million miles from that vision. All that was missing was Timmy the dog running alongside me, and a knapsack on my back containing a bottle of ginger beer and a brown paper parcel of jam sandwiches. I reached the island's heliport, which also doubles up as a cricket pitch, and took Appletree Road past the Abbey Garden and the monument overlooking Tresco Channel to Plumb Hill. This was the hottest and longest part of the journey. Kevlar jackets are not made for cycling in on hot spring days.

It is odd enough, just walking around one of the off-islands on-duty. For any member of the visiting public who happens upon us, the sight of policemen in full uniform is always incongruous with the surroundings. Absolutely everyone, other than the locals, does a double-take every time. There is clearly nothing in their minds that can compute the idea that firstly there is a police officer on one of these idyllic islands, and secondly that we are on foot patrol – both such a rare sight on the mainland that the majority of people are compelled to comment on it. I like to put on my matter-of-fact 'Oh, this – I patrol here every day' face. But inside I'm giving myself a high-five for having the best policing job in the world. And that's just when walking. Riding a bike, and in particular a child's bike, takes this whole unbelievability to another level. I am certain there were people I passed who had to sit down by the side of the road after I had gone, to wonder if they had just seen what they thought they had seen.

At Plumb Hill I cycled on past the Great Pool into New Grimsby. As I drew level with the New Inn, with the harbour to my left, I saw in the distance, about 200 yards away, a friend I knew from St Mary's. He was just getting into his small wooden boat from the granite steps at the end of the quay and untying it from its mooring.

I rang my bell furiously and shouted to him, to get his attention, and pedalled faster to reach him, before he started his engine and would be unable to hear me above the sound of his two-stroke outboard.

'Chris – Chris! Can you get me to Bryher?'

He heard me and indicated with a wave that he would wait, while I pedalled even faster to show that I was willing myself not to delay his plans. At the steps I dumped the bike, with the back wheel still spinning, and hopped into the little punt with my next captain. Chris whisked me across the 400-yard channel of water that separates the two islands, to Anna-Quay at Bar on Bryher. He didn't ask what the rush was and just matter-of-factly helped me out, as everyone before him had. I reached the island fifty minutes after setting off from St Mary's. I had journeyed to three islands, been on two boats and a child's bike in that time. Even if I did not catch my man, it was a hell of a day out.

Whereas Tresco feels several decades back in time from St Mary's, Bryher is yet another decade back in time from Tresco. Basically it was as if I had been transported back to the mid-1950s. The charms of Bryher cannot be understated. On one side of the island is a calm coastline that runs alongside the shallow blue waters of the channel. On the other side is Hell Bay, which, as it sounds, is rugged and wild, where the full fetch of the Atlantic slams into it during storms. Fewer than eighty people live permanently on the island. There is a pub, Fraggle Rock, the Vine Café, a post-office-cum-grocery-store, a chandler's, a fishmonger and several art shops scattered around the island. At the incredibly beautiful Hell Bay itself, there is a hotel – rather unsurprisingly named Hell Bay Hotel. The roads are crude, sometimes no more than compounded dirt or sand. In other places the march of progress has taken over and, like all the off-islands, rough concrete roads are laid down over time, yard by yard, by the locals laboriously mixing one load after another in a regular cement mixer.

Dotted all along the roads outside the homes are charming honesty boxes, which define their cottage industry. Little unstaffed boxes, barrows or crates, sometimes lovingly painted, offering up for sale all manner of locally made produce and trinkets. A purchase relies on honesty. You take what you want to buy, and leave payment in the jam jar or tin at the stall. You can buy everything from handmade vanilla fudge to hand-picked fresh crab, beetroot to books, trinkets made of painted limpets to full-sized canvas paintings. With a few hours to spare, you can graze your way happily around the island and leave with an armful of souvenirs, yet not have spoken to a single shopkeeper. It is a system that is seldom abused and that further adds to the ambience of no crime. Shame, therefore, that someone was prepared to dent that record with a spell of drink-driving.

I had a hunch I would be best placed to intercept the driver at the road that ran past the bottom of the church. I thanked Chris for the ride and he puttered off down the channel back to St Mary's. I was on my own again, and yet another leap removed from back-up support, if this plan started to crumble. I headed off along the high-tide line of the soft sand at the top of the beach for the short walk to Church Quay.

It is worth mentioning at this point that whenever I am on patrol, I do have my police radio with me, burbling away in my earpiece. I can hear all the broadcasts from officers in West Cornwall, dashing anonymously in their panda cars from St Ives to Redruth and then on to Penzance from one job to the next, all linking in with each other with ease. Arresting suspects and taking them double-crewed to Camborne custody centre, or taking statements from distressed victims, then moving on to the next job and the next, until an hour beyond the end of their shifts. Relentless, heroic effort from colleagues I may never meet, but whom I can hear going about their jobs with great professionalism and care for each other. All of this drama is playing out in my ear, wherever I go on-duty. Like all officers, I can switch into listening or switch off from it, but am always ready to respond to the sound of my particular call sign.

Although I work mostly in a veritable paradise, without constant demands on my time, I do envy my colleagues their camaraderie and their variety. It can be somewhat lonely, always policing on my own. I am sensitive to the risk of becoming out of step with the increasingly exacting standards, techniques and priorities that are being followed by all officers away from the islands. Some weeks, the only people I speak to outside my immediate family are those I am holding to account for their misdemeanours. I say 'on my own', but actually I am forgetting the 60,000 people who follow some of my exploits on the social media platforms that I manage on Twitter and Facebook. These folk have generated their own pro-social culture, particularly on our Isles of Scilly Police Facebook page, and while I may be the current master of ceremonies, it is often the case that I simply open the conversation with a light touch-tale of Scilly villainy, and then stand back and am entertained with where they take it.

People are marvellous and kind. Some of those not from Scilly I have now met personally, and I would go so far as to say that they have become familiar, friendly acquaintances. In four years I cannot think of a single bit of trolling of any note. If I get something wrong or am unclear, I am put right, but in a very tolerant and patient way. If I make a spelling mistake, it is picked up on and I am ribbed for it. When I get something right, the fun starts and the levels of humour that people come up with keep me chuckling for weeks. When matters I am dealing with mean that I have to get serious, people are respectful of that.

Our Facebook page keeps me sane, and I am deeply indebted to each and every one of the people who now make up our own canteen culture, be they from amongst the 2,200 residents of Scilly or the remainder of the world. It is a culture where cakes and cats feature highly, and people compete to come up with the wittiest retort to one of my posts. Apart from the odd urgent story that I blog, all my writing is done off-duty, outside my shifted hours, and not in paid time – as, indeed, is the case in writing every word of this book. I enjoy introducing people to my working world and showcasing Scilly, which I am deeply fond of, and where I have now lived for longer in the same house than in any other home in my life. I'm still the outsider, though, and I do not forget that. An expat who will move on. Living and working on Scilly as a police officer is not a career-long vocation. At least not in my view, and I think I can speak authoritatively on this, being the longest-serving officer here for several decades.

With the woes of West Cornwall playing in my ear, I completed the last bit of my journey across yet another bit of stunning scenery to the next idyllic quay, where I reasoned I could lie in wait, to make this my potential crime scene. All my ducks were in order that day. I had taken exactly one hour to get to my intended destination, and within two minutes of arriving the driver showed up on his quad bike. He had a hitch-hiking child of no more than six sitting on his lap. I stepped out onto the road and hailed him to stop. The exact details of the procedure I followed are not really that important, beyond the court. He failed the breathalyser test and was clearly unfit to drive, so I arrested him there and then on the sandy track by the beach. We looked at each other and he must have been thinking the same as me.

'Now what?'

I had to get him back to St Mary's before too long, as for every minute he was with me, his eventual blood-alcohol reading would be lower. I wasn't going to have made that journey for nothing, and now I was under the gun to do it all the way back to St Mary's. I didn't fancy having to give him a piggyback on Isaac's bike from New Grimsby to Carn Near.

While I was fathoming out what to do, the gods smiled on me again and sent yet another boat down the channel, piloted by a man I knew well enough to have his mobile number on my phone. I called him and, after a brief conversation and understanding the fix I was in, he came over to the quay and collected us both and ferried us to St Mary's. The rest is pretty much the tale of an ordinary drink-drive offence. The driver's blood did indeed show a result over the limit and he was duly prosecuted. The secret agent who passed on his concern to me was not involved in the prosecution, and I hope fully appreciates the genuinely good deed he did that day. This is not about the particular person who was drink-driving, for he has since served his debt to society. It is about how we are motivated to act, when we are passed the right information. There are five pairs of eyes and ears on Scilly employed by Devon and Cornwall Police, but it takes the remaining 2,195 pairs of residents' eyes to look out for each other, too.

I'd ride a child's bike every day to catch an offender, given the choice – perhaps not on the mainland, but in a location such as Scilly it doesn't seem so out of place, on reflection.

THE GROTTO

In early December, the head honcho of the Parent Teacher Association of the local school gives me a phone call. Above the din of the Christmas records on the radio, the chair of the local PTA asks us at the police station, almost formally, if we will help out at the Five Islands School Christmas Fayre. They need us to supply police officers for the grotto.

We are not being asked to supply reinforcements because of a perceived security risk; it is a grotto, not a ghetto, and our threat assessment suggests there is a very low prospect of disorder or criminal conduct at the event. Drug-dealing and gun crime at this – the only school on Scilly, with just 250 pupils – is certainly at comfortably low levels. No, this request is for the police to supply a couple of us to act as Santa and his elf for a few hours. Our brief is to lurk in a yurt-like tent for several hours, in a room just off the receptionist's foyer. The room is decked out with fairy lights and fake snow. The grotto is made up of a gazebo with the legs shortened, so that at its apex it is just five feet high. It is impossible to stand upright, once inside. Every adult entering the grotto has to do it at a low stoop, or even on their knees.

Inside, Santa sits on a plastic child-sized seat borrowed from the school dinner hall. He is surrounded by cute, fluffy toy reindeers, polar bears and penguins, with a couple of different sacks to choose from, containing presents for the various ages of the children. The blind is pulled down on the only window in the room, leaving sparse lighting coming from several strings of cheap, pulsing Christmas lights, both inside and outside the tent. It is all designed to take on an igloo-like resemblance. It fails in that respect in every way, every year. Despite a hundredweight of white tinsel and flashing lights, it is a claustrophobic, sweltering cave in a dimly lit room. I feel more like Marlon Brando in *Apocalypse Now* than Tim Allen in *The Santa Clause*.

In the grotto, we witness a procession of virtually all children aged from infants to about nine or ten being dispatched to us from the furthest reaches of the islands. Accompanied by their parents, they line up in a long, snaking queue outside the room, eyes wide with wonder at the thought of meeting Father Christmas. The children are wide-eyed, that is. Actually some of the parents, too, but that probably has more to do with hanging around the food-and-drink stall, sneaking more than their fair share of mulled wine with the mince pies. The children's wonder starts the minute they enter the room, trying to figure out what all the fluffy white stuff scattered in drifts represents.

The mild maritime climate on Scilly very rarely offers up blizzards, or even light falls of snow. I would imagine that if you lived on the islands all your life, you could count on one hand the number of times you woke up to a white blanket covering the flower fields and heaths. Many of the young children will never have seen real snow, in the flesh. Even the southernmost edge of the glacier during the last Ice Age didn't dare trundle over the archipelago. It ended on the northern beach-head on St Martin's. Neolithic people used to go there to find fine flints on the island, which were pushed in the moraine ahead of the ice sheet. Even now, it is possible to collect glacier-scratched pebbles from the top of Great Bay. We don't know if those ancient inhabitants knew anything about snow, either, or if they had a name for it, but 5,000 years later there is still no word for 'snow' in the Scillonian dialect. Honest!

The elf collects the child at the head of the queue and navigates him or her with the parents to the door of the grotto. There is a bit of banter between the elf and the child beforehand – the warm-up act effectively. This helps with the early introductions. The elf is like the beautiful, slender-legged hostess on a TV game-show, minus the beauty and slender legs.

'Santa, this is Eleanor. She is six and wants the new Queens of the Stone Age album for Christmas.'

This introduction is partly for show, as we generally know all the children's names anyway, but we have to keep up the subterfuge that the child is unknown to us. We ask them questions about whether or not they have been good. It is not unlike the process we go through in custody, booking in prisoners, when we ask them if they have any cautions or convictions, knowing full well what the Police National Computer reveals about them; we just want to see whether or not they will 'fess up and tell the truth. The interrogation into what the children want for Christmas starts after we have fully discussed their good or bad character wrap-sheet. Unsurprisingly, all the children tell Santa they have been good that year, although the ones accompanied by parents do exchange nervous glances. We have a little chat about this dubious claim, without wrecking their expectations, in a quasi Santa-police type of way. Invariably all the children want some consumable that has been ruthlessly marketed to them on TV or YouTube, and which we have never heard of. Father Christmas then lets them delve into the sack to pull out a wrapped gift. The accompanying parents and carers frequently take mugshots of their child sitting next to the main man and his sidekick, and the job's a good 'un.

The training for this role was not extensive, although if it were a function run under the direction of the Home Office, I expect a Grotto Management Course could be strung out for a full half-week to a week, with mandatory yearly requalification. 'Give them a present each, and their seasonal fix of the magic of Santa' is the basic remit that we are given, and I think we manage to deliver on that. It is not lost on us that for the rest of the year we actively look to dissuade children from talking to strangers, let alone entering their homes and accepting gifts from them.

The PTA always gets quick and enthusiastic confirmation from us on the phone that nothing would please us more than assisting them with this policing task.

We have done this gig for several years. It is, however, a dubious pleasure for at least one of us – the one who has to be the elf.

Both the costumes for the roles are dug out of the grown-ups' dressing-up box at the school. The traditional Santa cloak, trousers, hat and beard are pretty standard fare. Santa even gets the prop of a swag bag of presents. There is a great deal of anonymity to be gained in hiding behind the big white beard and Santa is never recognised. The obscurity of the bushy facial hair makes this particular role in the partnership the plum one. The elf costume, however, bares all. A little green waist-length tunic, jaunty floppy hat and large Dr Spock elf-ears are flatteringly set off by green tights and curly-toed slippers. There is nothing to hide behind and, as mature, hairy-legged blokes in our late forties, wearing the tights makes this role crushingly embarrassing.

The PTA supplies the costumes and the presents for the children and builds us the grotto. All we have to do is decide which one of us plays which role, and how we are going to get there. In the normal course of events, Santa would arrive pulled on a sleigh by Rudolph and his mates. It is not the absence of a sleigh that makes this impractical for us on Scilly, but it is a fact that even when we are handing out presents to the children we are still 'on-call' and have our radios with us, ready to respond in our official capacity, if required. This might be a call for us to go to any part of St Mary's (or, indeed, any of the other islands) for any incident under the sun. Relying on a lichen-munching reindeer to get us somewhere fast is probably not going to be the best plan in an emergency, despite claims for the reindeer's ability to circumnavigate the globe in a single night.

As it happens, our professional services have never yet been called upon while performing this Yuletide function. Perhaps this is a small blessing. I have speculated on how the person in need of police assistance would react, were they to see a big fat bloke in a red cloak with a beard – accompanied by another hefty bloke with pointy ears and green tights – turn up barking the phonetic alphabet into their radios to investigate the crime. Probably unfavourably. Of course there is the prospect that this festive uniform could actually be of benefit, should there be, say, a fight in a pub. Rushing into one of the locals inns, for instance, and confronting drunks, while dressed as the festive duo, might confuse and distract them for sufficient time to be able to get the handcuffs on and make arrests. I may even suggest this as a policing initiative to Headquarters, now I'm thinking about it. Then again, it would inevitably result in the compulsory Grotto Management Course.

The mode of transport to the school gig is obvious and inevitable. Santa is driven by the elf to arrive at the school in the police Land Rover. Which one of us is detailed to be the driver is not down to hierarchy. The elf has to do the driving, because Santa's ample cushion-padded gut gets in the way of the steering wheel. Perhaps this is why he generally travels everywhere by sleigh, which provides more room between his bench seat and the 'Dasherboard'.

The transport is only one of two considerations. The

other is: who does what role? Remember: nobody wants to be the elf. There are three ways this could be decided:

1. The role could be shared in alternate years. The problem with this is that, as police officers, we are not posted to Scilly permanently. The general rule of thumb is that between the three of us stationed here, one of us will leave each year and go back to the mainland to police. That person is then replaced by another officer from the mainland. In that way, there is some level of continuity for the policing of Scilly. A spin-off is that the privilege of serving on the isles is shared, as well as it can be, amongst the three thousand police officers of Devon and Cornwall Constabulary. Spreading the jam thin, but increasingly less so as police numbers shrink. Divvying up the role of the elf and Santa in alternate years would quickly go out of sync, and would disproportionately advantage and disadvantage one of the three of us. There are complex algorithms at play here. Option 1 would lead to disgruntlement, and perhaps valid grievance claims. I suspect lesser things have ended up in employment tribunals.
2. Flip a coin. This is by far the fairest method. Heads you are Santa, and tails the elf. This idea has merit and it is difficult to argue with, which is precisely why we do not argue about it and instead settle for Option 3.
3. I pull rank. I have the most senior police rank on

Scilly, and that should suffice. The sergeant is *always* Santa.

That has been the understanding for all the years that St Mary's Police have performed this function under my supervision. I am Santa, and I get to hide behind a big white beard. One of the other two Police Constables is the elf and has the ignominy of being recognised in tights. The stripes on my shoulder were hard-won and mean I don't have to showcase my legs in sheer green tights or wear the stupid pointy ears. Look at it from a logical perspective: if somebody were to call the police on Christmas Fayre day, and we turned up in costume and I was not Santa, imagine the confusion. Dressed as the elf, I would be the one seen to be calling the shots, telling my elder and better what to do. Everybody would think Santa was incompetent – drunk perhaps. It could shatter people's confidence in both the police and the magic of Christmas. It would be a scandal and a farce that might bring down a great institution. It has to be that Santa is boss and, as I am boss, I am Santa.

So that is how that particular bit of assistance to the PTA is organised and staffed. Pretty straightforward and simple, really. Over the course of two hours we meet and greet upwards of ninety children, then retire to our polar retreat at the police station. One year we turned up and there was a children's football match on, next to the school. In full dress, we ran onto the pitch and Santa joined the red team, as an obese centre-forward, with the elf playing wing for the greens. Ten minutes of being the one all the little cherubs wanted to tackle left me wishing I had padding on my shins, as well as around my ample paunch. These were the same children who, an hour later, would be sitting next to me telling me they had never been bad. The bruising on my legs told a rather different story.

Contrary to Noddy Holders' assertion on the radio that everybody is having fun at this time of year, this is a period when, as any copper knows, there is a spike in arguments and domestic disputes. It is a time of greater stress, when a year's worth of unresolved issues come to a head, there is greater alcohol consumption, and families are forced into different patterns of behaviour and spend more time with one another.

Scilly is no different in that respect. We get calls from couples, when emotions boil over and the red mist comes down, just like everywhere else. I'd go so far as to say that, in my view, the couples who actually get us involved make the best of a bad deal and come off better than those who don't involve us. We are not hell-bent on taking action against either one of the partnership, unless harm has been done or a clear risk exists that it will be done in future. It is about doing the right thing and supporting the couple with the help their relationship needs, at that moment in time. Both Mat and I are fathers and know all too well that it is also about focusing on the welfare of any children in the partnership, and ensuring the parents do, too. For the duration of my career I have never heard a colleague refer to such an incident as 'just a domestic'. It saddens me when I read sloppy journalism or hear scriptwriters who perpetuate this stereotype of the police. I feel the language used says more about the commentator's perception of the problems than it does about the subject itself.

And so it was that, one evening in early December shortly

before a grotto unveiling, Mat and I got called to one of the islands, to assist a couple who were involved in a disagreement at their home. Heated words had been exchanged and there was an impasse. Fortunately there were no offences, and nobody was complaining of having been harmed. It was a verbal exchange, on the way to an inevitable divorce, which had not yet escalated beyond hasty, hurtful words. As a priority we went to the room of their child and checked on the little one, who was sleeping soundly in the bed. The infant had slept through the whole drama, probably dreaming peacefully of the excitement to come at the School Fayre the next day. With the child safe, we were left to negotiate a truce between the parents. We talked through the issues with the unhappy couple and saw to it that there was unlikely to be a resumption of hostilities, before taking our leave. One parent was sleeping elsewhere for the evening, while the angst cooled. Sometimes it really is as simple as that, and all parties are left with a better understanding of where the other's boundaries lie – both theirs and ours. It still took several hours to manage, though, and we were happy to be part of the solution at a low moment in their relationship.

The next day at the grotto saw us all meeting up again, in entirely different circumstances. About halfway through the seemingly never-ending line of customers, the elf pulled back the snow-door of the dingy tent to introduce the two selfsame parents we had counselled only the night before, along with their now very-much-awake child. It came as an unanticipated emotional experience for all the adults concerned, when we met in these distinctly different circumstances. This time they came into my world. The juxtaposition of the situation with that of the night before was apparent to all four adults.

'Santa, this is Annie! She is five and wants a My Little Pony for Christmas.' I could hear the crack in the elf's voice as he delivered his introductions, his memory still fresh with the knowledge that Annie's world would probably change soon, in a way she could not yet comprehend. He remained professional throughout, both as elf and as police officer, and was successfully keeping up the subterfuge.

The little girl came into the room and sat on the child's seat next to me. She gazed about in wonder at the lights on Santa's sack and at the soft toy penguin (when were there ever penguins at the North Pole?). Her parents knelt a few feet in front of us, with their heads hunched into their shoulders, to keep them from poking into the low-slung roof in this dimly lit, cramped hovel. It felt uncomfortably as if they were kneeling before me in shame. It was like I was a high-court judge – strange beard instead of strange wig. There was an awkward hush that felt as if it lasted a lifetime, but in reality probably lasted less than a second. Were all of us thinking, 'What happens next?' The four grown-ups exchanged sheepish glances, and then the elf departed.

I felt my larynx tighten, so I sucked in a deep breath to avoid delivering my well-rehearsed lines in a high-pitched un-Santa-like squeak. Relaxing into the part, I affected my deep voice and turned towards Annie.

'So *you* are Annie. It's lovely to meet you. And you have brought your sister.'

She looked at me with a look of withering incredulity, as they all do. 'That's not my sister, that's my mum.'

'Oh, I see. And you've brought your granddad, too.'

Now seeing the joke, but necessarily putting me right, she responded, 'That's not my granddad, silly, that's my daddy.'

'Oh, I see. He's had a hard paper round, hasn't he?'

I looked back at the parents. This bit of flirting, in plain sight, generally breaks any awkward tension. It gives the power to the child. The parents were smirking; the ice was broken. We were going to survive and make a decent fist of it for the child.

I delivered the 'Have you been good this year?' question, and it felt as if I was asking more people than simply Annie. Even though I wasn't looking at them, I sensed a brief wince from each of her parents as I quizzed her. Annie assured me that she had been good all year, and as she had not been one of the hooligans that I had been assaulted by on the football pitch earlier, I had no reason to doubt her.

Uttering my spiel, I offered her a present from the sack for the older children. The really young ones – the ones who are too young to have a clue what is going on – get a book. The older ones get a variety of trinkets, which I feel duty-bound to tell them is not their main present. I will deliver that on Christmas Eve, but only if they are sleeping.

In another small twist of irony, I had my mugshot taken with the child, before the family took their leave of my abode.

That afternoon the elf and I saw another eighty or so children in the grotto (some of the visits having an occasional underlying subplot), then drove back to Garrison Lane to get out of our ridiculous sweltering costumes and put on our more standard-issue sweltering Kevlar jackets and helmets.

Maybe next year the elf and I will get called away from the grotto to do the easier stuff, like breaking up a fight in a pub.

A WINTER'S TALE

After making a stiff coffee, the first job in the morning is to check the answerphone. I know it is generally now known as voicemail, but in the context of Scilly that is inaccurate. The 'mail' part of this modern name tends to imply that an address or number is included, or at least some indication of who the caller is. It makes getting back to the person who phoned a much easier task. There persists a presumption on Scilly that everyone knows everyone – and that evidently includes voice recognition. Many presume that we will simply know who they are, without them leaving a name or number. It is both charming and frustrating in equal measure, and can stretch our detective skills to the max. We are, to my knowledge, the last police station this side of Pluto to continue publishing our telephone number. We do this so that people can call us direct. But the first few hours of the morning can be spent simply figuring out who left messages, let alone dealing with their concerns.

Back in March 2015, still glugging my last sip of coffee, I reached for the playback button. The metallic voice of the machine announced its tally of messages: 'You have THREE new messages. Press ONE to hear your first message.'

I pressed one and waited, ready with my pen to scribble down the details.

'Message left at EIGHT THIRTY-SIX P.M., on THURSDAY, TWELFTH of MARCH. Number withheld.' Beep!

'Hello, it's me. We're holding a hop, skip and jump down The Strand in April for the children. Would it be all right if we borrowed some cones, please?' Beep!

I wrote the message down without the faintest clue who the message was from or how to get back to them. I'd decipher it later.

Next.

'Message left at ELEVEN FORTY-THREE P.M. on THURSDAY, TWELFTH of MARCH. Number withheld.' Beep!

'HELLO . . . HELLO! Is there anyone there? Why aren't you there? There's shouting in the street outside. All sorts of noise going on. I can't sleep. Why aren't you out on patrol? Where are you? Huff!' Beep!

I took a risk and made a working hypothesis that as the message had been left more than nine hours previously, the shouts had been from the last drinkers as they dragged their way home after the pub. We get these messages left sporadically. Double-demands that we should be both at the end of an answerphone and out on patrol. It makes for an interesting take on omnipresence. There would have been an alternative for the caller, of course. We try repeatedly to persuade residents on Scilly to use 999, or the non-emergency 101, but somehow an indignant diatribe left anonymously on the telephone vents the spleen so much more robustly.

Next.

'*Message left at* SEVEN FIFTY-EIGHT A.M. *on* FRIDAY, THIRTEENTH *of* MARCH. *Number* ZERO-ONE-SEVEN-TWO-ZERO-FOUR-TWO', etc. Beep!

'Hello, message for Colin. Colin, it's Park House here. We just wanted you to know Mary is not very well. She's gone downhill overnight. She's resting in her room, if you want to see her. I'm sure she would love it if you came over.'

Park House is the island's rest home. It is a great example of what a home for the elders of a community should be like. It is not tucked away and hidden, like an untended corner of the garden. This home is in the centre of town, along Church Street. The main lounge window is set right along the pavement, with a view of all the comings and goings up and down the street. I like to pop in for a chat and a cup of tea every so often. More people should, really. They would learn stuff – I have. There is a lovely atmosphere in there that is widely recognised and appreciated. More than once I have heard the middle-age generation musing in the street, only half-jesting, 'I've already booked my place at Park House.' It carries no stigma, and they do make exceptionally good tea.

The message I had just heard put me in a heavy-hearted mood. Mary was one of the long-term residents I was particularly fond of. She had been getting increasingly weak for a while and her end was near. I'd be flattering myself to think I had any significance for her, but for my uniform. Even so, that thought did not concern me whatsoever. I enjoyed, with simple affection, the rapport I had with Mary and the effect that my uniform had on her. For the latter years of her life, every day was a new day. Her formative years were the ones that were prominent in her thoughts, and these were from decades before I was born. Going to see the residents at Park House was always an increased pleasure for me when Mary was up, awake and sitting in the day-room. She was always the first to speak to me when I entered the lounge where she and her fellow residents sat during the day. I might not spot her at first, but I could feel her eyes burning into me. The exchange between us was always pretty much the same.

'My father was a policeman in the war.'

'Where was that, Mary?'

'Milton Keynes. They add up to ten, you know.'

'What do?'

'Those.' And she would point to my epaulettes, with the number 4501.

'The numbers on my shoulder? Four-five-zero-one?'

'Yes, ten.'

'I guess they do.'

'Can you take me home?'

'Yes, Mary. Where do you want to go?'

'Jacksons Hill. I've been here a few weeks. I need to go home.'

'OK. I'll have my tea first.'

She seemed satisfied with this and would hold out her hands for me to take. When I held them, they were always much warmer than mine, which had just come in from outside. I'd sit beside her and drink my tea, chatting to everyone else while Mary sat contentedly next to a police uniform, lost in the memory of her father. It filled her with evident content: a man who did the same job as me, but in very different circumstances in a different era, during the Second World War. My presence clearly gave Mary comfort, and that made my visits all the more worthwhile.

Mary's exploration of my epaulette numbers was curious. I missed the significance of it for years. Her superior intellect still shone through, though, despite her inability to express it, beyond the small, easily missed clues. Clues like the fact that she could beat all the contestants on *Countdown* at the Conundrum, while only distractedly watching the TV. This was a mere trifle to her, occupying her increasingly complex mind while in tick-over mode. I knew little about Mary until her last days.

There was a sunny, warm day in spring the year before when I paid her a visit. She seemed agitated at not being able to go out and enjoy the fine day. I decided to extend our lounge-bound relationship with the offer of a walk around town. I asked her carers if it would be OK for me to take Mary out in her wheelchair, if she wanted. When I put it to her, she was very enthusiastic about the prospect. The carers dressed her in warmer clothes, we helped her get into her wheelchair and put a beige checked blanket over her legs. I took the handles and pushed her out of Park House into a sunny afternoon in May and turned left to go to the promenade at Porthcressa beach, a short stroll away. Me in my full uniform, stab-vest, handcuffs and pepper spray, my radio burbling, wearing my custodian helmet, and Mary in her blue Fruit of the Loom fleece with a tartan throw on her lap. I had hoped that her mood would improve with the sun on her face.

After only a few yards she rather curtly made it known to me that I was taking her in the wrong direction. She wanted me to take her home. I shrugged and turned the wheelchair around and pointed her in the direction of Park House. This made her instantly angry. 'Where are you taking me?'

I was only eager to please and didn't want to anger her further. At that time my own father was in a nursing home in Devon, bed-bound and locked in the advanced stages of dementia. My remoteness from him meant that I was unable to travel to him frequently and support my mother, who visited him daily. I would have loved to be able to take him out for a stroll with me in the sunshine. Like Mary, he was mostly confused about his place in time and space.

I knew that before taking up residence at Park House, Mary had lived on Scilly at Jacksons Hill, which was in the opposite direction from where we were heading and half a mile away. She had lived there for many years. She was known affectionately as the 'Cat Lady'. She fed a menagerie of cats – strays that lived around the large council yard at the bottom of her road. The cats congregated there because this was the site at Morwell where the islands' household refuse is dumped and mounds up, awaiting a cunning plan to deal with it somehow. The 'Morwell Alp', as it is infamously known, has a resident population of cats. Mary's passion was painting and caring for them.

'I'm taking you back to Park House. Is that where you want to go?'

'No, home.' There was an impatient intolerance in her voice.

'Jacksons Hill?' I queried.

'No, NO, man. Wavendon.'

'Wavendon. Where's that?'

'Wavendon. Wavendon – Buckinghamshire. Take me home.'

With rising panic, I pushed her wheelchair in the direction of The Strand, where I could show her the harbour and explain the impossibility of the brief she had given me. Wavendon was a forty-mile ferry crossing and a 300-mile drive away. I had serious doubts we would make that by the end of my shift. Added to that, we were drawing attention from onlookers. Some were close enough to hear our conversation and were amusedly sympathetic to both our causes. Others, too distant to hear our exchanges clearly, were watching what they could only presume was a moment of over-zealous policing, as an elderly invalid lady was presumably being arrested, much against her wishes. To Mary's evident disgust, I gave up on the 300-mile gentle stroll to Wavendon and we returned back to Park House, having been out for less than fifteen minutes. Wavendon would have to wait for another day.

On the morning in March 2015 that I got the answerphone message, I made it a priority to see Mary. I took with me some police reports that I had to read, and sat quietly in her room alongside her while she rested. It was as good a place as any to work on them. Mary was unable to speak by this stage, and I could not be sure that she even knew I was there. I noticed there was a little blue box on the bedside table, open and displaying its contents. It contained a single medal. Curiosity got the better of me, so I peered closer. It was evident that her carers had placed it at her bedside, keen for everyone who visited her to see it, to reveal the character of the lady who could no longer speak, lying next to it.

I read the inscription on the medal and the penny dropped. Now I fully understood Mary's brilliance and why she could beat all the contestants and the *Countdown* clock; the deciphering of my shoulder number; and the significance of Buckinghamshire. I cursed myself. *Listen to the clues, Colin, they were there all along. Clues in the things said and done, which reveal the person within.* My insight into this fading elderly woman beside me became instantly richer. All preconceptions about her living just a simple life on a small island, known to everyone affectionately as the 'Cat Lady', were gone. Yes, that was who Mary was, too, and very much by her own design, having had a much more complex life beforehand.

'FOR SERVICES TO BLETCHLEY.' The brief script that went with the medal recorded that Mary worked at Block D, Bletchley Park, in Buckinghamshire between 1944 and 1946, in the German Navy, Army and Air Force Enigma Processing and Decryption Section. The work of Mary, and people like her, is credited with shortening a terrible war by several years, and without it the outcome for millions of us would have been uncertain. I have since been led to understand that it was Mary who sent out the coded message for the D-Day landings. After the war she took a top executive position in the top-secret British Intelligence communications centre, GCHQ, in Cheltenham. She was very modest about her career and, after retirement, moved to Scilly where she looked after and painted stray cats.

I sat with her for as long as my duty permitted, feeling in awe of the lady who had managed to decipher what the massed ranks of the Third Reich were up to around the world, and yet I could not outwit a couple of fuel thieves siphoning off petrol from local punts in the harbour. Mary Winter, MBE, hung on to life until early the next week, when her nephew managed to make it to Scilly to be with her in her final hours.

A week later, as a mark of respect, I attended her funeral at Old Town Church in my full dress uniform. I'm sure Mary would have appreciated it. I miss her, but I still very much like to go to Park House to take tea. I try harder now to listen for the clues giving an insight into the other remarkable elderly friends I have made there. As was the case with my father, some of the residents suffer from dementia – a disease that, in my experience, takes a family member long before they actually pass away. To miss a person while they are still with you brings grief. Many of those I have met in the care home are people I did not know before they became so afflicted. Consequently I find that I have nothing to miss about them, and everything to learn from them. My relationship with them is not tinged with sadness. I suspect that every time I visit it is like meeting me for the first time, for some of them. They may not know me, but they do recognise the uniform and come from an era when it was universally respected, and it is plain to see that it sparks warm memories for my friends there.

Daphne Chudleigh insists that I sit with her now. I'm only just learning about her, in dribs and drabs. She too has warm, soft hands. Amongst other things, I have learnt that she used to take afternoon tea with Tommy Sopwith, when she worked for the aeroplane manufacturer Hawker Siddeley in London in the 1940s. She flew their planes on occasion. She hasn't yet been able to tell me precisely which variation of the single-seater Hurricane she piloted.

HIBERNATION

Policing Scilly is full-on or full-off. There is little in between. For the seven months of spring to mid-autumn it can be very busy, despite popular perceptions. November to the end of March tends to be considerably slower. There are far fewer people here, and consequently fewer calls for our services. Virtually no tourists visit. Perhaps a few look to stay with relatives, but on the whole the place has a very different feel about it. This is when all those odd jobs get done. The Land Rover gets sent back to the mainland for servicing, and we get a replacement car sent over on the supply ship, the *Gry Maritha*. These winter months can drag, both on- and off-duty. There is little by way of entertainment: no cinema, no theatre; there is a great museum along Church Street, but even that is not going to fill those long winter months. I'd go so far as to say that I prefer being on-duty in the winter, as rarely is there a day when I will not go into the police station, just to find something to do. This would be a great place for someone to embark on building a scale-replica of the Eiffel Tower out of matchsticks.

There is enough to fill our day at the police station.

Firearms checks keep us busy all year, along with our work with the school, driven by PCSO Shirley Graham, in the delivery of a significant part of their Citizenship curriculum. In spring each year we take the whole of year-group nine, the fourteen-year-olds, for what we call the '999 week'. We spend a full week with them away from school, introducing them to all manner of citizenship skills, such as an understanding of how the courts work, safer relationships, and drug and alcohol awareness. Remember that these are children who have predominantly lived only on Scilly. In many respects they grow up quickly, with levels of independence and autonomy that many mainland children will not have. Their play involves roaming far and wide across whichever island they live on, and by the time they are in their early teens, some of them are extending their play to other islands. There is a palpable lack of fear here. In other respects, Scilly children are very under-exposed to risk factors that mainland children learn to manage at far younger ages. Traffic awareness is one aspect. There are no traffic lights or pedestrian crossings on Scilly, and only one roundabout that I can find, and that is on Bryher. With the greatest of respect to residents of that island, the roundabout is only there because there is a palm growing in the middle of the road.

In November we take the same year-group, now in year ten, to Penzance for the week. We introduce them to a richer gambit of policing skills: Traffic, Firearms, Dogs and Divers, along with a trip to court and input from the Crown Prosecution Service. The highlight is invariably the cinema on the Wednesday, and the curry on the Thursday. The students enjoy this trip, too. These are things they can't get on Scilly.

For the most part, though, it is very quiet out here in winter. It can be pinpointed to the very moment when Scilly goes into shutdown mode and hibernates. The *Scillonian III* sails from the end of March to the last Saturday of the autumn half-term holiday in early November. The horn on the ship blows as she pulls away from the quay, on her way back to Penzance for the last time in the year. These four blasts from the ship signify both that she is under way and that winter is, too. If you are on the ship, you are off to a part of the world where you will see people, movement, entertainment, restaurants, shopping, culture and distraction. If you are left on the quay when the horn sounds, God help you if you struggle with your own company. The ferry is not coming back to offer you a passage to escape for another five months. The only realistic option then is to fly.

Close-down means that most of the private boats are out of the water. With mild interest, we all keep an eye on the craft left on their moorings or running lines, to see whether they will defy the rough weather of the winter and remain afloat. Even the calmer waters of the harbour can be rough when the wind blows from the north. The running lines are a cunning method for mooring a boat afloat, consisting of a sixty-yard-long loop or rope tethered to the dry harbour wall at one end, and submersed around a heavy sunken chain running parallel to the shore at the other. A punt can be tied at any point along the length of this line, and pulled back to the shore when needed. Stern to the shore, it has a fair chance of riding the waves as they hit it. Tie it bow to the shore, and the transom at the stern takes the brunt, and more often than not the boat will fill and sink or turn turtle. A few forgotten small craft are claimed by the sea most seasons, their hulls washed up or sunk on Town Beach.

The likes of the big orange RNLI lifeboat, the *Whiteheads*, stays out on its moorings all year round. In pole position at the entrance to the harbour, she pokes her bow out into the open sea and benefits less than the other boats from the sheltering effects of the quay. There is nothing but open ocean between her and Newfoundland, 1,700 miles due west. Winds and heavy swells between all points of the compass north-west to north make this forty-tonne vessel strain at its moorings like a rearing stallion. Other main players of the harbour are the bright-yellow ambulance boat, the *Star of Life*, the grey-blue medical launch, *Vanquish*, and the harbour master's jet boat, the *Pegasus*. They all stay afloat year-round, but are tucked in a less-exposed spot further into the harbour. All of these boats play a part in our policing in some capacity.

The *Star of Life* is our boat of choice in an emergency, should we need to get to one of the off-islands urgently. It is an odd-shaped, bright-yellow boat with a catamaran hull. The rear cabin is kitted out just like the inside of an ambulance. It is a lifeline to those who live on islands other than St Mary's. The skipper's phone is on speed-dial on our mobiles. One call and we can rely on either of the two Martins who share the job of sailing her to get us, in a hurry, to any island. She remains an ambulance boat, however, and once we are delivered safely onto the quay at the island of our latest drama, she returns to St Mary's harbour without us, leaving us stranded to do our business and make our own way back. *Pegasus* and on occasion

Vanquish run us back and forth between the islands at times of less drama. All of these boats are highly seaworthy and their skippers are supremely able, even in the worst conditions.

The restaurants, hotels and accommodation-providers are mostly closed at this time. Stoically the Star Castle sticks it out until just after New Year, and then it too pulls up the drawbridge and hunkers down for the remainder of winter. The whole feel of the place is different. Many local people have left the islands for extended holidays or to stay in their mainland homes. The seasonal staff for the hospitality industry have all left. Many of those who frantically saved their wages for the last month head off to the sun, to party it up in Thailand for the southern-hemisphere summer. It is mass migration for many, leaving what feels like a skeleton crew behind to look after the islands. An evening patrol during the week can see us count maybe four or six people in each pub. That includes the staff. Little chance of a public-order incident. I'd go so far as to say it is desolate.

Were this the prairies of the Midwest USA, there would be tumbleweed. We have our own equivalent, though. The kelp and bladderwrack seaweed that grows long and rapidly in our clear waters breaks from its rock anchorage at this time of year and is washed up on the shore by the ton. Some of the drier bits get wind-blown down the streets: tumble-seaweed. The beaches turn from crystal-white fine sand to dark-brown sludge. The air gets thicker with the smell of the mineral salts of iodine, potassium, magnesium and chlorine. What would be an eyesore in the summer is a bounty in the winter, for this rotting algae is a great soil-enhancer. Allotment-holders drive their cars onto the beaches and pitchfork hundredweights of the stinking free stuff, to spread on their soil. It rots down well before spring, if done early enough, ensuring good, healthy crops of vegetables in summer. There is no point in the council clearing the beaches. The sea will eventually run to a high spring tide and reclaim the rotting algae that the gardeners did not get to.

When the tide does this, there is another bounty to be had. If the tide that washes the beach clear in winter co-incides with calm weather, the sharper fishermen with boats at the ready at the top of the beach lay nets in the bays. Putrefying kelp is manna for fly-maggots, and these in turn – when dragged into the sea – are food for the grey mullet. These elusive fish come into the coves on the high tide and scavenge the shallows, looking for what the sea has clawed back from the land. A well-placed net can catch a haul of mullet worth exporting. These three-pound fish are good eating here. On the mainland they are often returned to the sea, if caught, as their meat tends to be muddy, for they feed on estuarine silt. Here there are no estuaries, no rivers running off into the sea. The water is clear, and consequently the mullet meat is fresh and sweet.

MAY THE FITTEST SURVIVE

In the event any of my successors read this, before arriving to take up their post on Scilly as the sergeant, I'll offer no real guidance on how to survive here. Even though it could be said that there is indeed an element of survival on the rock. By 'survival' I am not talking about the likes of scavenging for food, although my memory serves to remind me of the many times I have been into the Co-op to find the shelves virtually devoid of fresh food. The sort of supermarket food shortages not seen east of the Iron Curtain since the Berlin Wall was torn down. Our wall is the ocean, which sometimes gets too rough for the supply ship to cross and replenish stocks. These are the moments when survival-of-the-fittest does take over. It is that moment when two shoppers, equidistant from the last-remaining onion for forty miles in any direction, simultaneously spot it on display. Momentarily, time stands still. They shoot each other steely glances, challenging the other to go for the vegetable first, before they snap out of it and gritted-teeth politeness kicks in. There follows a game of 'No, you; no, you; no, I insist', before the more European of them wins, and the self-sacrificing Brit goes home empty-handed.

But for a matter of a nanosecond, I almost found myself in this position on 24th December last year. I had been dispatched on an emergency errand to purchase the one item we had forgotten for the big meal the next day – carrots. As I made my way through the shop to the virtually empty shelves of the root-vegetable section, an elderly couple who were shopping together got there a Higgs boson half-life ahead of me. I arrived at their shoulder just in time to hear the husband turn to the wife and say, 'Look, dear, the last carrot on Scilly. This will be a lovely Christmas Day treat for the ponies on the Garrison.'

So yes, there is an element of survival-of-the-fittest out here, but I am not really talking about the Bear Grylls stuff. You may never need to resort to drinking your own urine. People have not had to scavenge limpets off the rocks and chew on these rubbery molluscs for many years. Possibly not since Neolithic times, and probably not again until a cordon-bleu restaurant comes to town with fancy ideas. The middens of the Neolithic peoples who lived here 6,000 years ago are still easy to see. They are the equivalent of their landfill sites, where they discarded thousands of limpet shells. They can be seen exposed in the eroded cliff at Porthcressa below the allotments, if you don't believe me. I like to take my children there when they complain about having to eat cabbage or liver, to talk to them about variety. The survival that I mean is more about career survival.

You will do it your own way no doubt, but for pointers on how *not* to go about things I offer just one suggestion.

Consider watching *The Wicker Man*, the 1973 cult folk horror movie with Edward Woodward. If you are unfamiliar with the plot, I'll offer a brief synopsis. The main character, Police Sergeant Howie, is sent to the remote island of Summerisle. To cut a long story short, he didn't keep his ear close enough to the ground to hear the sound of the lynch mob coming up behind him and ended up being burnt alive, inside a huge wicker man, while the islanders fanned the flames. The significant element in this plot is the May Day celebration, and Howie's suspicion that the community had been planning a sacrifice to the pagan gods all along, to ensure a good harvest. The criteria for choosing a sacrifice, he discovered, was that the chosen one should arrive voluntarily, have the 'power of a king' and be a fool. The islanders picked a young girl as the May Queen. The sergeant made the unsound presumption that the child would be the sacrifice, but alas, that was not to be. It was he who fulfilled the necessary criteria and was therefore set alight. It is a ripping yarn that features amongst the best of horror films; a bit dated perhaps, but well worth a night in with popcorn.

Of course there are no huge similarities with Scilly, so perhaps I should not have mentioned it. The open copulation in public between the islanders, which was depicted in the film, is almost non-existent here. At the very most, you will need a decent halogen torch and fresh batteries to pick out the writhing bodies on Porthcressa beach after midnight on a hot summer's evening. The 'power of a king' criterion was taken in the movie to be met, as Howie was a lawman, a bit like us. Well, exactly like us really, but a coincidental link not worth losing sleep over, in my opinion. The Summerisle residents are famed for having a rich harvest, which a conspiracist may try to convince you is similar to the renowned flower farms of Scilly. Rubbish – put it out of your mind. Perhaps I should not have mentioned it at all. It could never happen here. I'll write about something else that is unrelated.

Imagine our joy when our daughter, Bella, was chosen as the May Queen in 2015. I am led to believe that her name was picked from a hat perfectly randomly. The May Day celebration is an ancient tradition, going back many, many decades. There are photographs from the turn of the last century, showing this ceremony taking place even then. It is a ceremony put on by all the school-age children up to the age of eleven. They are all dressed in white, from head to toe, both boys and girls. A maypole is erected in the Parade park, with colourful tassels hanging down. A stage adorned with thousands of flowers is built for the May Queen and her attendants to sit in state on, while rounds of complex songs are sung. They dance around it and sing songs for the best part of an hour. A very charming, yearly top-up of a quasi-pagan life here.

It was standing room only, around the park. Everyone watches – locals and visitors alike. Many of the local people who were themselves part of the ceremony many moons ago still know the words and sing along with the children. The occasion oozes charm. Even the burly tarmackers, who were laying down the new road surface nearby, put down their noisy tools, switched their steamrollers off, lent on their shovels and stood watching the dancing while the ceremony was in full swing. They hummed along with the catchy tunes, like almost everyone, while beads of sweat ran down their dirty, tanned faces, enchanted by the spectacle of innocent happiness playing out before them. Then they got back to the boiling tar for a couple of hours, before reminiscing about their childhoods over ten pints of lager in the evening.

We police play our part in this tradition. Our role is to escort the snaking procession of children, with their garlands and flowered staffs, through the town from Carn Thomas down The Strand to the park. This is one of those occasions every year when we get into our number-one uniform: the tunic and best heavy woollen trousers, topped off by the best helmet with the nipple on the top. The tunic is a very smart piece of police clothing. In my opinion, the black Police Sergeant tunic is far superior to any other tunic worn by any other rank from Chief Constable down. The heavy white chevrons on the upper arms just nail it. I love wearing it, but as it is a fitted jacket it is next to useless as an operational garment. There is nowhere to carry a radio, or any of the other clobber we heave around. When I joined the police, I was also issued with a pair of ceremonial white cotton gloves. It was my understanding that I only wore these in the presence of the Queen. Nobody actually specified which queen, so I took it to be any queen and wore them when escorting the Queen of the May and her attendants. It can all feel a little Old Empire, a back-in-time experience. A bit like the early 1970s, now I come to think of it. A bit like Sergeant Howie's time.

TICKETS, PLEASE

Can I just put to bed a well-circulated policing myth, once and for all. If my whole career is for this one moment, it will have been worth it. There is no law that states that a pregnant woman can pee in a police officer's helmet.

This is all bunkum. I am not legally bound to offer up my helmet to anyone. There is no modesty to be preserved in standing bow-legged, clamping an upturned pith-helmet between one's thighs. The woman would have to be so drunk to consider that a dignified option, that hospitalisation and an urgent referral to social services would swiftly follow any short-term relief. There is also the simple fact that it gets hot under that helmet, so to improve ventilation it has holes in it. Upside-down, the hat is basically a sieve. It has more use as a device to drain pasta than it has as a bedpan. If you really want to wee on your shoes, there is absolutely no merit in straining it through my hat first.

Sadly, at pub closing time, it doesn't stop the same person asking me week after week, month after month, year after year, 'If I was pregnant, you'd have to let me piss in your hat, wouldn't you?' To which my now well-rehearsed and weary line is, 'No, I wouldn't, but if *you* were pregnant, I'd let you. However, you have some considerable hurdles to overcome first, Daniel.' I do wish he would stop asking, or man-up and get pregnant.

I raise this because we get asked it a lot here. Spending so high a proportion of our time on foot patrol means that we have to deal with disproportionately more inane queries into the folklore of policing than police on the mainland do. Daniel and his mates account for a sizeable proportion of these inane questions. The frequency of these requests reaches a crescendo by the end of the year. New Year is special in this respect, because it is the one evening on which I and my colleagues are not the only ones wearing costume. It is a tradition on Scilly, as it is in many places, to get dressed up in fancy dress to do the pub crawl. This tradition is as strong as ever here, although perhaps the numbers of people involved are yet to return to those seen in the 1990s. Then Scilly was very much the place to be, and was cited alongside Trafalgar Square and Rio as the places to see in the New Year.

We are the last place in England to see in 1st January, and are on the same latitude as Dublin in Ireland and Stornaway on Lewis, in the Western Isles of Scotland. Not that anyone really cares what time the first day of the year starts. We certainly don't. This is a bank holiday, and we generally only work on such days if there is something pressing on. This made it all the more curious when on 2nd January one year I went back to work, to find a deluge of complaints against us for being over-zealous on New Year's Day. Apparently many of the cars around town had been given what the drivers took to be parking tickets on 1st January. As the only people who can issue tickets, we were accused of being over-enthusiastic, especially on a bank holiday.

I scratched my head and asked my two colleagues if they had had a rush of blood to the head and had got so bored at home that they took it upon themselves to put penalty notices on cars. They hadn't, of course. Then I saw one of these notices. They were clearly rubbish forgeries. Not even that – just yellow bits of paper with 'Parking Notice' photocopied on them, and a New Year's greeting. From a distance and at a squint, I suppose they could have been mistaken for tickets, but only by people who had never seen the unleashing of a full-on parking-enforcement campaign. They were the work of a fancy-dress reveller on New Year's Eve. A local man had dressed as a traffic warden and had ticketed all the cars in town. He had been very effective, I must say. I applaud him for his work ethic, and if he would like to make himself known to me, I will be more than happy to offer him a job.

FINALLY

I have the courage of my own convictions to profess an antipathy towards A-line skirts. I can pinpoint it to the exact time when I developed this aversion forty-four years ago – a spring tide (the name of the tide just after a full moon where there is the greatest difference between high and low water) in the summer of 1972. I was six years old. I can even tell you the names of the two women who wore these skirts and made this perfectly innocent item of women's wear raise the hackles on my body. It was two women whom I saw only fleetingly, at a distance of fifty yards, and have never seen since. Babs and Evelyn Atkins were their names. They were sisters, who only eight years earlier had upped-sticks from suburbia and purchased Enys Lann-Managh, the Cornish name for the island a mile offshore from Hannafore Beach in the town of Looe. It is more commonly known as Looe Island or, as my nana called it, St George's Island.

All holidays were spent with my nana at the beach at Looe. As a child, I could see the island a mile out to sea directly off the beach, ever-present as the main feature through her lounge window. I grew up with it featuring on my horizon, quite literally, as the greener pasture I wanted to get to. It made a great impression on me. As a child born in the 1960s, the stories of Enid Blyton's Famous Five and every adventure of Hal and Roger Hunt that Willard Price ever wrote featured dominantly in my imagination, too. They were read to me at bedtime by my mum. The stories and the island became blended into one, in my psyche. This was compounded when, one spring tide in the summer of 1972, my father took me and my younger brother Martin out for a walk. Not any old walk, but one with an adventure in it. We were to race the super-low spring tide on a scramble out to Looe Island, across the exposed rocks, have an explore around and come back in time for saffron buns in the afternoon.

As on Scilly, there is a very large difference between high and low tide at Looe, which is even more marked on a few spring tides every year. On these occasions, the sea retreats to such an extent that for a few hours it is possible to get out and back to the island before the tide turns, to flood back in and close the gap until the next low spring tide. It does this, too, on Scilly between all the inhabited islands, apart from St Agnes, which has a deep-water channel between it and St Mary's. On just a few days each year confident walkers who are not fazed by getting a little wet can make the journey on foot from Bar Point on St Mary's to St Martin's, then from there to Tresco and on to Bryher and the uninhabited Samson island. The faster walkers can make the return journey too, but by the time they are on the last leg back to St Mary's, from where they started, the sea will be flooding back in. The last bit is done wading neck-deep, for the stragglers.

The walk to Looe Island is shorter and less varied than the route around the archipelago here. On Scilly the sea has risen to cover over Neolithic fields with submerged granite walls and standing stones. Millennia ago, many of the islands were connected as one. Then the sea levels rose, relative to the land, and divided up the single mass to form multiple islands. When we set off for Looe Island in the early 1970s there was no great crocodile of marine ramblers taking advantage of the super-low tides, as is the case now, both here and there. When we embarked on our expedition it was just me, Dad and Martin, in our swimming trunks. Dad calculated correctly that it would take about forty-five minutes beach-to-beach. The island grew larger and larger in my field of vision every time I looked up from the careful placement of my feet, as I waded through knee-deep water. Fat shrimps darted to the safe cover of the seaweed as we picked our way out through the rock pools.

My brother and I were young, and for much of the journey Martin rode on Dad's shoulders because, at just two years old, he was too short for the deeper pools of water. As we arrived at our destination and made our way out of the shallows, two women appeared out of the woodland at the top of the beach. They were that particular brand of middle-aged spinster that is easily mistaken for formidable schoolmistresses. From my perspective as a six-year-old, they were far more fearsome than the spear-waving natives Willard Price had implanted in my head. They looked similar to each other, but if asked to describe them further, I can only recall that they both wore green tweed A-line skirts, with pleats just below the knee.

Dad left me and Martin at the water's edge and went to make first contact with the women, to see if they were friendly. They were, but told him that, as the owners of the island, they charged a landing fee of two pence each. No money, no entry beyond the high-tide mark. Dad only had his trunks on and had not brought any money with him. Consequently our Island Adventure was over the moment it began, and so we turned politely on our heels and, disheartened, trudged through the kelp and bladder-wrack back to Hannafore. It was not quite the wondrous exploit I had conjured up in my mind, but at least the women had not fired poisoned darts at us. I was denied the quest that my imagination had convinced me lay in that mysterious place. I had not been able to be my hero Hal, Roger, Dick or Julian. It was not fair to a little boy of six.

Our failed venture to reach Enys Lann-Managh made such an impression on me that ever since that date I have had a passion for notching up islands and remote places. This is the one thing I think I can claim some consistent success at, over a number of occupations. Most numerously as a conservation biologist in the Indian Ocean, Shetland, South America and Norway, but most notably as a police officer here on Scilly. These islands offer somewhere in the region of 150 bits of rock that protrude above high tide. I'll never tick off all of these, nor will I try. Most are reserves for the abundant flora and fauna that we enjoy out here, and they appeal to my former career in conservation. The whole of Scilly is a designated Area of Outstanding Natural Beauty, a fact that is abundantly clear when you are out standing at a high vantage point.

For instance, St Agnes is home to significant populations

of Manx shearwaters. These birds were in dire decline and at serious risk of becoming extinct on Scilly. I have been fortunate enough to muscle my way in as a volunteer on a project to carry out conservation work on their rehabilitation. A significant part of the threat to their numbers came from rats. These introduced mammals were chomping their way through the chicks of the shearwaters, such that none were recorded as having fledged for many years. The rats, which were not historically endemic to the island, were removed from St Agnes and its Siamese twin of Gugh. Between them, these islands have successfully become the largest island mass in the world with human habitation from which rats have been removed completely. The people of St Agnes were the factor that made this happen. They saw their island for what it could be, and will now become. They welcomed the conservationists in, to roam scientifically across their fields for several years, monitoring, measuring and maintaining bait stations to clear the islands of the invasive rodents. The shearwaters started fledging chicks immediately – a fantastic success that, if maintained, will see Scilly become even more of an incredible wildlife spectacle in years to come.

I have come to view Looe Island, and all islands ever since, as synonymous with adventure. I like the boundaries they impose. What you have there is what you have, and with that you must make do. This is what is important about islands to me: the resources I can rely on, and the people around me, are finite. I enjoy maintaining a simplified mental inventory of all that is available to me, to complete a task or live an existence. When something is depleted or used up completely, there may be no replacing it. It will be gone for ever, if it was endemic to that island. This is just as true of the wildlife that I enjoy doing my bit to conserve, the people in the communities I am privileged to work amongst, and the cultures and customs that exist in these locations. I am very happy to have witnessed what Scilly has, in these respects.

My career as a police officer on Scilly is finite. By the time I leave I will have had the privilege of serving here longer than any other sergeant for several generations. I will move on to a different post and be a police officer somewhere else. Unlike the Atkins sisters, I am not sure where my next island adventure will be. The seemingly inconsequential childhood influence that they were blissfully unaware of, back in 1972, set off a chain of events that influenced me for the next forty-four years. Mine were positive influences, which have scarred me only to the extent that I have a wincing disregard for an item of women's clothing it is most unlikely I would ever have been drawn to wearing in the first place.

Had I been the child in the hand of his parent who was told to 'Behave, or the policeman will arrest you', or had I come from a household where the language around any mention of the police was full of negative slang, then I wonder how that would have played out in the scheme of things. How would it have been if I had been the victim of abuse? Would I have had the confidence to disclose my concerns to protectors or investigators? With the careless use of language, would doors have been closed to me unknowingly by others? I don't know, but what I do witness is that the children of parents who take the trouble to see beyond the uniform are far more confident and forthcoming, unfazed in the presence of a copper. They lend me bikes, they swap hats with me, they let me escort them to May Day celebrations and, when they are older, they want my company as they near their end. The children of parents who with a broad brush vilify the police are, in my view, doing no favours to their children. Consciously or subconsciously, they are cutting off their avenues of support.

A different sergeant for Scilly will pitch up after me, and another one after them. They will all see things with new eyes and will manage matters in their own way. They will move into the home that we have lived in, for a total of seven happy years. I hope they will all enjoy it as Sarah and I have. But more than that, I hope they don't resent us because of the dreadful lime-green paint in the bedroom.

POLICE REPORTS

Weekly police update from Isles of Scilly to Penzance Inspector:

Ma'am,

I have to report that we have received a complaint that somebody has forced open the door to the Football Club shed at the playing field next to Five Islands School. It is fairly evident that this was done sometime over Tuesday evening, and most probably to get a football out for a kick-around. Regrettably, however, the door was damaged in the process, with the bottom of the door split. Shirley and I attended the location. We could find few clues as to how this came to happen, other than a fried egg that was left at the scene.

I will be attending school tomorrow to ask at assembly if anyone knows anything about this. We are just looking for the person responsible to own up, and this can all be dealt with quite amicably, which is the request of the shed owners.

I have released a public message to the media of the salient points in the case. I'll summarise:

Low-key investigation with amicable resolution, if
    admitted.
A fried egg was left at the scene.

Other than that, all is well on Scilly.
Report ends.
Sgt C. Taylor

Weekly police update from Isles of Scilly to Penzance Inspector:

Ma'am,

Do we have permission to keep a cat at the police station? There is this large Russian blue that has pretty much adopted us. He is called Mowgli and doesn't do much, other than sleep in the detention cells all day. He seems to be a bit of a hit with visitors, and we are currently receiving several callers every morning at the front desk, just wanting to see the cat. I stuck his picture up on our Isles of Scilly Police Facebook page and he now has about 50,000 fans. We get post for him. Quite frankly, it would be difficult to see how we could get rid of him now. There would be a revolt.

I don't suppose a cat-flap on the steel door of Cell 1 would be in order, would it?

Other than that, all is fine on Scilly.

Report ends.

Sgt C. Taylor

Weekly police update from Isles of Scilly to Penzance Inspector:

Ma'am,

I have to report that there has been a report of damage to a car. The owner has stated that the nearside front wing of her 4x4 has been scratched, leaving multiple irregular marks in the paintwork down to the metal. I have taken some pictures of the distinctive tagging the offender has left in the car, in case this develops into a series of like crimes. There is no CCTV covering the places where the owner habitually parks her vehicle, on the road by her home or in her field. We have little to go on. The suspect may well remain undetected.

Other than that, all is well on Scilly.

Report ends.

Sgt C. Taylor

Weekly police update from Isles of Scilly to Penzance Inspector:

Ma'am,

Further to my message from last week, I am happy to report that the criminal damage to the car has been cleared up. The owner parks her car in her field while she feeds her animals. While she was doing so this week she heard a scraping sound behind her and turned to see the culprit, who she recognised. Her old blind horse was chewing the front wing of her car, leaving deep gouges that perfectly matched last week's scratches/tags. I have written this crime off.

Other than that, all is well on Scilly.

Report ends.

Sgt C. Taylor

Weekly police update from Isles of Scilly to Penzance Inspector:

Ma'am,

The November visit to Scilly of our soon-to-retire Deputy Chief Constable David Zinzan was a success. Well, sort of. I am afraid he wanted to go out on patrol with me, and it was a grizzly day. I made the mistake of taking him to Tresco, which at the time I didn't know my way around very well. The estate there were good enough to lend us push-bikes. We rode about a bit while he told me about his career as a senior officer in the Metropolitan Police and as head of the Flying Squad. I don't know the back-roads on Tresco very well and I'm afraid I got us lost in the mist. We got a bit damp. And muddy. He didn't seem to mind much, though, and said it was his best day on patrol in his thirty-one years of policing. The Flying Squad must have been grim.

On leaving us, I think the sea air may have made him a bit giddy. He has promoted station cat Mowgli to Deputy Chief Constable.

On the upside, I know Tresco like the back of my hand now.

Other than that, all is well on Scilly.

Report ends.

Sgt C. Taylor

Weekly police update from Isles of Scilly to Penzance Inspector:

Ma'am,

I have to report that I may have fallen out with a local resident. She admonished me while I was off-duty on Porthcressa beach. I went down to the water's edge to get rid of a bucket load of fresh mackerel heads and guts, from my catch earlier in the day. This attracted a huge flock of gulls, as would be expected. I have since learnt that this may have been against local rules. I got a proper scolding from a lady who lived nearby. She came out of her house and marched down the beach red-faced, shaking her finger at me. She was quite scary and very effective at getting her message across. There may be a complaint against police coming your way. If there is, please reassure her that I won't be doing that again.

I note that Headquarters have announced that they are recruiting for more Special Constables. We could do with another out here, as Special Constable Merryn Smith has announced his intention to retire, after ten years of sterling service. I think I may have identified a suitable candidate. Would it be in order for me to approach a lady who made herself known to me this week, and who displayed many of the right characteristics?

Other than that, all is well on Scilly.

Report ends.

Sgt C. Taylor

Weekly police update from Isles of Scilly to Penzance Inspector:

Ma'am,

I am excited to report that the Isles of Scilly Police Team, consisting of PCs Mat Collier, Marc Blyth and PCSO Shirley Graham, has won an award at a RNLI fund-raising event. They attended the multi-agency function with staff from the local Lifeboat, Fire and Rescue and Coastguards. There were many local people there too, to bear witness to the sterling efforts of all the different disciplines. It went on long into the night. You will be pleased to hear that, at the end of the evening, our police team was presented with 1st Prize in the Annual Emergency Services Pasty-Making Competition. We think it was Marc's inventive use of some pheasant-breast fillets that he had in his freezer, and Shirley's finesse at slicing turnip, that swung the judges' vote. That and the fact that the Fire crew stepped on the Coastguards' pasty and then added too much salt to their shortcrust pastry. Do I have permission to display the trophy – a knitted pasty mounted on a plate – on the office wall of the police station?

We will be competing to retain the trophy next year.
Other than that, everything else is well on Scilly.
Report ends.
Sgt C. Taylor

Weekly police update from Isles of Scilly to Penzance Inspector:

Ma'am,

I took much of the week off, as leave. I spent a very pleasant few hours sitting on the cliff at Peninnis, looking out to sea. Did you know that if one stands with one's back to the lighthouse there and looks out across the big rock directly due south, then the next landfall will be Bransfield Island in Antarctica, 8,600 miles away. Falkland is only 7,300 miles away, as the crow flies.

I will be back at work on late shift this evening, as I have done all my staring at the horizon for the week. I will be focusing my attention on things closer to home – like shouting rude stuff in the street, weeing in alleyways and riding bikes without lights.

I think everything else on Scilly is fine.

Report ends.

Sgt C. Taylor

Weekly police update from Isles of Scilly to Penzance Inspector:

Ma'am,

I have to report that the police Land Rover broke down twice this week. The first time the engine management system cut out. The garage here says it's because we don't drive fast enough, and there is not enough length of road for the engine to properly heat up. We have been advised to rag it in first gear at 5,000 revs up Telegraph Road on a monthly basis. I am afraid the throaty diesel makes a terrific noise, so there may be some complaints coming your way.

The other breakdown was a simple tyre puncture, which meant I had to pull to the side of the road in the pouring rain and fix it myself. Everyone who drove past honked their horn at me and grinned, while I was down on my hands and knees soaking wet, jacking up the car. I don't think they were full of solidarity. I know where they all live, though, so there may be some complaints coming your way.

Other than that, all is well on Scilly.

Report ends.

Sgt C. Taylor

Weekly police update from Isles of Scilly to Penzance Inspector:

Ma'am,

The fierce storms that have been hitting us all this week have abated for the moment. The ninety-mile-an-hour winds blew tons of sand off the beach and onto our roads. Many of the homes with windows facing the beach now have frosted glass, from the sand-blasting they received. Large bits of debris from the sea and beach were whipped up in the wind and deposited well beyond the high-tide mark. PCs Faye Webb and Mat Crowe were out in the worst of the weather, braving the gales. They used the police Land Rover to get the children living at Old Town safely home from school. Then they deployed into Hugh Town, where they helped out with the rescue efforts of the flooded buildings. I think they should be commended for a brilliant effort, in the face of some dreadfully heavy seas and strong winds. Especially as I had to order them to stand even further back from the water, when I found that Faye had a small fish stuck behind her police radio.

Other than that, the clear-up effort is going well on Scilly.

Report ends.

Sgt C. Taylor

Weekly police update from Isles of Scilly to Penzance Inspector:

Ma'am,

Could you extend my apologies to our Corporate Communications Department at Headquarters? I rather rashly put up a spoof job advert on our Facebook page, for the vacant police post on Scilly, then went on holiday away from Scilly for the weekend. The post went a bit viral. For a week the whole department at Corp. Comms was inundated, fielding requests from reporters and hopeful applicants from all over the world, including Italy, Greece, Texas, Australia, Germany and Spain. I think it somewhat distracted the department from their other work. To be fair, what was supposed to be our family trip back to the mainland turned into a bit of a fiasco, too. I spend much of my time doing radio interviews over my mobile with Spain, New Zealand, the UK and the US. Top tip, though: if you ever find yourself at the Premier Inn at Hayle, the place to get the strongest wi-fi signal and be guaranteed of a quiet place to chat to Radio 5 Live is the cleaner's cupboard just off the foyer. It is pitch-dark in there, and blow me if I could find a light switch!

There are no other matters to report from Scilly.

Report ends.

Sgt C. Taylor

Weekly police update from Isles of Scilly to Penzance Inspector:

Ma'am,

Two matters this week. They are as follows. You may be delighted to note that an abandoned baby thrush that we were caring for briefly in Cell 2 has successfully fledged and is now living independently. The detention room is no longer a temporary aviary.

Additionally there was a visit by Her Majesty's Inspectorate of Constabulary. Two senior officers descended on us at short notice to conduct an inspection of our Custody Suite. They seemed broadly pleased with what they found. I sensed that despite the Chief Superintendent's evident love of animals there may, however, be one small advisory note in any report they produce. Herewith I am withdrawing my request for a cat-flap on Cell 1.

You will no doubt be relieved to note that I report these two events in chronological order.

Other than that, there are no matters to report from Scilly.

Report ends.

Sgt C. Taylor

Urgent police update from Isles of Scilly to Penzance
Inspector:

Ma'am

I appear to be a few police cones short of a promising
career. It is looking touch-and-go for me having enough to
mark out a convincing No Parking zone for the royal visit
today. In hopeful anticipation of surviving this crisis with
my job intact, I have issued an emergency public notice
that I would request you to read and retrospectively approve.
It consists of two elements:

1. Please do not park adjacent to Holgates Green
   this morning. No nonchalantly nudging-apart the
   sparsely separated bollards with your bumpers,
   just to make a car's length to squeeze into.
2. Running alongside my heartfelt plea for civilised
   parking, I am proposing a Cone Amnesty. If you
   have 'borrowed' any for 'projects', please can we
   have them back? Typically they may be found
   lurking in garages, gardens, teenagers' bedrooms
   and Methodist Church Hall car parks. If they
   come back within the fortnight, we will spare you
   even the Paddington Bear stare. We can also play
   along if you want to maintain that you have just
   found them. If you do locate any, let us know or

bring them to the police station, where I may or
may not still be working. Thank you.

I have taken the liberty of releasing this message to the
community.

Other than that, there are no other matters that are
likely to seriously limit my career aspirations.

Report ends.

Sgt C. Taylor

Weekly police update from Isles of Scilly to Penzance Inspector:

Ma'am,

In an effort to boost our statistics, I have started publicly arresting local people on spurious charges and releasing their interviews to the media. To date, I have arrested both the Church of England chaplain and the Methodist minister, the bus driver and a lobster-fisherman, our cleaner and the chair of the local council, and at long last Terry Ward of the Foredeck and his father. I have extended this service to non-islanders, too, and have further arrested the Police Crime Commissioner and the Deputy Chief Constable. In total I have increased our arrest figures significantly and now have twenty-six otherwise upright citizens released on bail.

If I may be permitted to explain, I have done this under the guise of an hour-long slot on local Radio Scilly in a show I am calling *Criminal Records*. I interview, under Caution, one suspect a week, to a list of set questions, exploring their answers to such questions as:

- You can have someone informed that you are in custody. Who would you like us to contact, and why them? (This can be any person, alive or dead, fictitious or real.)
- You were searched when brought into custody, but

I see that you have smuggled an item into the cell with you. What is it and why did you smuggle that item in? (This can be any item, large or small, however implausible it may have been that you smuggled it past me. It cannot be anything to assist your escape or to cause harm.)

- Your rights include being able to read a copy of the Police and Criminal Evidence Act 1984 (PACE). I will allow you another book or reading material. What do you want to read and why?
- You can have something to eat and drink of your choice. What do you want to eat? (You can choose anything, although if you specify alcohol, I will have to ask you for a second choice, as you are in custody, remember, and this is a dry cell.)
- If you could be anywhere else in the world right now, other than in custody on St Mary's, where would you wish to be and why?
- When I release you, I may need to consider bail conditions. These can be things that you must or must not do. I'll allow you to devise a bail condition of your own that I can impose upon you. What will that condition be?

I intersperse the questioning by playing records of the suspect's choice, from the questionably owned MP3 player they had with them when I booked them into custody. The format seems to work very well indeed, and I have people actively asking to be arrested. I have additionally come to the conclusion that anyone with any form of policing connection has very dubious tastes in music.

May I be permitted to arrest politicians and celebrities who wash up on these shores?

Other than that, it is winter out here and the prospect of more meaty investigations is a distant dream.

Report ends.

Sgt C. Taylor

Weekly police update from Isles of Scilly to Penzance Inspector:

Ma'am

I have to report an injury on-duty. Strictly speaking, it is a Police Accident (POLAC) involving a vehicle. I was speed-gunning cars today near the school, when I was hit a glancing blow on the hand by a car. The owner of the vehicle was trying to go as fast as he could and clearly had no regard for my safety. I am not badly hurt, although my right hand is sore to the touch. I will be able to continue work without taking time off.

I have taken action and spoken to Mr Morrell, the science technical assistant at the school, who was leading his class in a physics experiment at the time. I will wear padded gloves next year, when I assist the class measuring the speed of their compressed-air-propelled toilet-roll dragsters. At a top speed of 21 k.p.h. they do bruise.

Other than that, there are no further matters to report from Scilly.

Report ends.

Sgt C. Taylor

Weekly police update from Isles of Scilly to Penzance Inspector:

Ma'am

This week I have had complaint of the theft of a limb from a pirate. The left tibia has gone missing from the skeleton of said corsair, which was on display on top of an aquarium. Its whereabouts are unknown. I am suspecting that skulduggery was at the root of this. I have taken steps to secure the evidence, where possible. I have my suspicions about who may be involved, but I don't think they will stand up in court.

Other than that, there are only some lame matters I have to deal with, which I will not trouble you with.

Report ends.

Sgt C. Taylor

Weekly police update from Isles of Scilly to Penzance Inspector:

Ma'am,

You will be glad to hear that the firearms amnesty has gone well. We have had several heirlooms handed in by people grateful to be offloading their weapons at long last. This has included a captive bolt gun, a Colt .45 with live ammunition, several air weapons, shotguns and a starting pistol. Amongst the items brought to the police station was a spud-gun. It was in its original wrapping, which says that it fires 'Harmless Potato Pellets'. The packaging also has a picture of children on the front, playing with it. The person who handed it to us was concerned it might fall into the wrong hands. I am grateful they did not bring all the ammunition they could find.

I have had the weapons taken to Headquarters for destruction. I did not send the spud-gun, however. Can I dispose of it here on Scilly? The school may be looking for raffle prizes for the summer fete.

Other than that, there are no further matters to report from Scilly.

Report ends.

Sgt C. Taylor

Weekly police update from Isles of Scilly to Penzance Inspector:

Ma'am,

I have to profess that I am getting a little cheesed off with the parents who see me in the street and tell their young child to behave or 'the policeman will lock you up'. Invariably the child will be doing nothing more devilish than holding their mum's or dad's hand. The parental warning serves only to potentially scare the child and reduce its trust in me.

I met such a family today and, when they warned their child in this way, I knelt down and told the toddler not to worry, as they were well below the age of criminal responsibility and had my permission to play merry hell, if they wished. I then gave them a badge and carried on my way.

I have taken to sharing my helmet with any child who waves at me with the polite number of fingers.

Rant over, and there is no more to report from Scilly.

Report ends.

Sgt C. Taylor

Weekly police update from Isles of Scilly to Penzance Inspector:

Ma'am

I would like to request some leave away from the islands. I think I must be suffering from a little stress and am starting to confuse fiction with reality.

A few weeks ago I finished my late shift at 2 a.m. I returned back to the police station from a quiet night of uneventful foot patrol, to book off. As I arrived at the front door I looked down and at my feet on the ground was a live goldfish. It was twitching, and clearly in the last stages of suffocation. I administered first-aid by dunking it in the sink and jiggling it about a bit. You will be pleased to know that it has recovered.

Today I returned to the police station after an afternoon's foot patrol in the company of another officer. On this occasion there were two goldfish gasping for air, directly outside the police-station front door. I was able to instruct the constable in the correct CPR methods for carp, and again you will be pleased to know that both recovered. All three fish have been rehoused.

Even though I have a witness, I am starting to become paranoid that I may be the subject of some form of Piscean stalker, hence the request for some time off.

Other than that, there are no matters to report on Scilly.
Report ends.
Sgt C. Taylor

ACKNOWLEDGEMENTS

If there is any truth in the suggestion that there is a book in everyone then I can now confirm that, certainly in my case, it has taken quite a mob to not only beat it out of me, but also piece it together to present as evidence to a jury of readers.

Literary Agent Tim Bates of Peters Fraser and Dunlop (formerly Pollinger) took my case on in the first instance. He and his team gave me the encouragement and confidence to pursue this to trial by publication. I am indebted to him for the way he enthused me to venture into an unfamiliar court in the first place where others left me unconvinced. He put his brilliant detective skills to great effect in dovetailing me with the very best editor in Ajda Vucicevic of Century. From the outset she has been the most calming, motivating and supportive encouragement I could ever have wished for. I recognise that she is also the author liaison officer fronting up a very professional team at Penguin Random House and I am equally indebted to the likes of Charlotte Bush, Sam Deacon and Sarah Ridley for their enthusiasm. Natasha Nel has been the superb artist who designed the cover and tolerated my pedantic requests for minute changes with apparent glee. I am also grateful for the interest editors of other publishers showed in me writing for them.

Social media has a lot to answer for in this disorder. Between the applications of Facebook and Twitter, a crowd of over 60,000, from all over the world, amassed over several years to read and jeer me on with my frequent blogging. In a shameless effort to pass the blame and increase my word count I would now like to thank each and every one of them personally. Firstly to Lisa . . . [*I'll stop you there, Colin. Editor* A.V.]. Seriously though I am genuinely humbled by the people who have become regular readers of the Isles of Scilly Police Facebook page and my @ScillySergeant Twitter feed. The way in which the crowd have gathered and continue to riot in a very pro-social way has been an inspiration to my writing. My blogging drew the attention of the press on numerous occasions and without exception I have genuinely appreciated the way in which the various journalists and features writers have been generous to me. In particular though four journalists stick out in my thanks: Genevieve Roberts of the *Independent*, Steve Morris of the *Guardian* and India Knight and Tanya Gold for the pieces they wrote about me in *The Times*.

There are no identity issues with this case. I produce this exhibit in my own right as Mr Colin Taylor. That said, I have appreciated the way in which Devon and Cornwall Police trusted me when I applied for permission to write outside of my job as a sworn officer of the law. The book is not endorsed by the organisation and any failings in it are all mine and mine alone. It was my corner to fight my way into and will be mine to get myself out of. I feel very proud to be able to call myself a Devon and Cornwall Police Officer and even more so now. I am particularly appreciative of the support of retired Deputy Chief Constable David Zinzan, who not only promoted a cat above me but also gave me great encouragement to write. There are other senior and junior rank officers and staff still serving who I have also very much valued the support of but I will not name them while they are in service. There is a remarkable bunch of people dedicated to protecting the vulnerable in the peninsula of these two counties. For me, the most significant in my case have been the small cavalry that I have had the privilege of working with on Scilly. In alphabetical order, I would like to thank Marc Blyth, Mat Collier, Mat Crowe, Shirley Graham, Nic Gould, Tess Lloyd, Merryn Smith and Faye Webb for their humour, professionalism and tolerance of the occasional multiple social-media pile-ups I have got us into. Inspector Jean Phillips who will be the one detailed to take me to task if this all goes horribly wrong which is why I have made this thick enough to slip down the back of my trousers if I am due lashings. I know they have rolled their eyes at my 'press briefings' more than is healthy for their optic nerves, but they really are a sterling bunch of people and have had my back. Scilly has been very lucky, I feel.

Scilly has also been the arena for this mêlée and with it the population, who have certainly given me the impression that they support their local sheriff. There are a few people I would particularly like to thank for their vocal support. In no particular order: Clive Mumford for his council, and Beth Hilton and John McKenzie of the *Scilly Now and Then*, who encouraged me to contribute monthly to their most excellent magazine. Thanks too to Keri Jones of Radio Scilly for letting me play Radio DJ with *Criminal Records*, which helped to galvanise my own desires to communicate beyond just shouting at drunks urinating in alleyways. My family would also like to thank Liz Clements for letting me hole up in her empty holiday let at Fairview, Moonakers over the winter to sit and write this book. This got me out of the house so they could continue to carry on as normal rather than tip toe everywhere to avoid disturbing the peace.

Without doubt I would not have been driven to these depths if it had not been for the support of my fantastic family. My mother, Julia, and truly wonderful wife, Sarah, have stood by me and will continue to as I rehabilitate after this ordeal.

I'd like to take each and every one of the people above named or otherwise out on a boat for an afternoon's fishing as a token of my appreciation, but sadly I fear I do not have enough rods and there can never be a boat big enough.